How to Win a Job in Educational Leadership

Insider Tips and Trade Secrets to Help you Score Your Goal

by
Dr. Marilou Ryder

©2012
Dr. Marilou Ryder

ISBN: 978-0-692-01696-1
Library of Congress Control Number: 2012933699

Disclaimer:

The Publisher and the Author has made every attempt to provide the reader with accurate, timely, and useful information. However, given the rapid changes taking place in today's economy and job market, some of our information will inevitably change. The author makes no claims that using this information will guarantee the reader a job. The author shall not be liable for any losses or damages incurred in the process of following the advice in this book. No warranty may be created or extended by sales or promotional materials. The advice and strategies contained herein may not be suitable for every situation. This work is sold with the understanding that the author is not engaged in rendering legal, accounting, or other professional services. If professional assistance is required, the services of a competent professional personal should be sought. Neither the Publisher nor the Author shall be liable for damages arising here from. The fact that an organization or website is referred to in this work as a citation and/or potential source of future information does not mean that the Author or Publisher endorses the information the organization or website may provide or recommendations it may make. Further, readers should be aware that internet websites listed in this work may have changed or disappeared since this work was written and when it is read.

Delmar Publishing
Huntington Beach, CA

In an effort to support local schools, raise awareness and funds, Ryder and Associates donates one percent of all book sales for the life of this book to:

Victor Valley Make a Difference Fund

Get involved today!
Visit: http://hdcfoundation.org

Publicity rights:

For information on publicity, author interviews, subsidiary rights, contact Ryder and Associates: 760-900-0556

or email
Marilou@Ryder-Associates.com

Visit our home page at:
www.ryder-associates.com

Also by Marilou Ryder:

The SeXX Factor: Breaking the Unwritten Codes that Sabotage Personal and Professional Lives
New Horizon Press, 2003

Go to the Head of the Class
The School Administrator, October 2009

Superintendent Gets Taken for a Ride
The School Administrator, February 2009

Cultivating Women Leaders through a Network
The School Administrator, November 2008

Create Your Own Aspiring Administrators Symposium
Leadership Magazine, 2006

Moving on Up: Promoting At Risk Students
Leadership Magazine, 2002

The Impact of Male Gender Dissonance on Women's Potential Eligibility for Advancement to the Position of Superintendent
UNI Dissertation Services, 1999

CONTENTS

Are you being granted interviews when applying for advanced positions of leadership?

Does your cover letter and resume stand out in the crowd and show paper screeners you're ready for the job?

Are you aware of the wide range of questions asked in interviews?

Are you prepared for the challenges of the high stakes interview environment?

Are you tired of coming in second?

Do you have a professional mentor?

Do you know how to inform your immediate supervisors about your plans to move up?

Do you know how to ask for stellar recommendations from key people?

Do you know how to accept an offer of employment?

Do you know what to do (announcements, resignations, etc.) once offered a new position?

Do you know how to negotiate salary or an employment contract?

Are you prepared to make mistakes and learn from them?

Do you have the time needed to prepare for and deliver a stellar interview?

Do you have the resiliency to withstand rejection and keep applying for the positions you want?

Parting Shots

Why Hire You?
Parting Shots
Interview "Do's"
Interview "Don'ts"

Champions
Real People
Real Inspiration
Coaches' Quarters
Parting Shots

RULES OF THE
GAME

Introduction

WHY YOU SHOULD READ THIS BOOK

The Comfort Zone

"Life begins at the end of your comfort zone."
~ Neale Donald

In 1986, I was happily working as a teacher for a school district located in a small suburb of Syracuse, New York. My world was shaken when my husband, in the throes of a midlife crisis, wanted to move his photography business across the country. I had settled into my job as a 5th grade teacher in the same school district I attended as a student. My high school history teacher was now my faculty "buddy" and I couldn't imagine my life being any better. I loved working with old friends and enjoyed teaching in the same classroom where I learned my multiplication facts as a third grader. Never much of an adventurer, my heart skipped a beat when my husband decided we should move to California.

I shared my dilemma with a friend who taught with me across the hall. "My God," she responded, "I can't even pick out new kitchen cabinets without having a panic attack. How the heck can you move across the country?" My sentiments were confirmed.

"We aren't going anywhere unless two things happen," I exclaimed. "First, I have I to find a teaching job and then we have to sell our house. That's the deal," I declared. "No job, no house sale… no California." With these two obstacles in place, I wasn't too concerned about leaving my comfort zone.

In January, I called at least ten different school districts to request teaching applications (there was no internet). For several days, applications were delivered to my home, and I spent hours filling them out by hand and sending them off in the U.S. mail. I wasn't enthusiastic but nonetheless, I had made a deal with my husband. He was excited about the prospect of moving to California, a lifelong dream he shared on our honeymoon. In early February, four districts called for interviews. I gasped for air. The only educational job I ever interviewed for was my current job. Our plan was becoming a reality and was gaining a life of its own. In April, we took a Red Eye to Los Angeles, booked a hotel, rented a car, and I began interviewing for California teaching jobs.

The teaching interviews that ensued could best be described as awkward. On all four occasions, only one person managed the hire; either a principal or a district office person. They asked me to describe my teaching style and probed to determine my fondness for children. I was astounded by their eagerness at the end of each interview when asked, "When can you start?" Much to my husband's advantage, California was in the middle of a teacher shortage crisis. Within a week, three calls came in with job offers.

I remained calm, since our agreement with one another included the sale of our home, and if it didn't sell by June, we would stay in Syracuse. With job offers in hand, we hired a realtor to place our house on the market. Our real estate agent was new to the business, which I thought was a good thing, believing that a rookie couldn't sell our house in time to meet our deadlines. On first inspection, the agent raved about the design of our house, the hardwood floors and unique, open living spaces. "I need to tell my son about this place," she reported. "He will just love it." When our realtor's son purchased our home the following week, the reality of moving to California as a 'life-changing' event was upon us.

Money Talks

I accepted a teaching position in Long Beach Unified School District, based purely on salary—$15,000 more than my current Syracuse salary and $8,000 more than the two other California districts that wanted me. When I asked Long Beach what grade I would be teaching, a woman on the phone said I had three choices: "Sixth grade, sixth grade or sixth grade?"

Since I had already signed a contract, I replied, "Well, I guess I'll take one of those sixth grades," and was assigned to an inner city elementary school in North Long Beach.

I met the principal a week before school opened and was quick to communicate to her that someone had made a big mistake. "There are thirty-six desks in my classroom," I explained. "Who can I ask to help me move them out?"

Her head flung back in laughter. She patted my shoulder. "Poor thing," she chuckled, "there's no mistake. This is California, my friend. You will always have 35-38 students in your classroom, and if one of those seats ever goes empty, it won't get a chance to cool off. We'll send in a replacement student."

Moving to California in the mid '80s from the East Coast was a lot like moving to a foreign country. Everything was different, from the way people dressed to the number of Mexican restaurants that seemed to be on every street corner. My students were multicultural, bilingual, and severely below grade level. I had difficulty transitioning to this new climate, sweating like crazy one day and freezing the next. California was unlike anything I had ever experienced. Teaching non-English speaking students and working in a classroom people referred to as a "bungalow" was some strange new territory for me.

Hmmmm? I was beginning to think I had made a big mistake coming to this high paying, inner city school district. I had no experience teaching inner city students and entertained the idea that I might not be able to handle my new assignment. One feature of this new job, however, fascinated me—the principal was a woman. There were no women principals in Syracuse.

Not for the Faint of Heart

It wasn't until a magnitude 6.2 earthquake (my first) that my principal recognized my leadership potential. After the quake, teachers were directed to march their classes out to the blacktop. What a strange sight to behold—1,000 plus students standing on the asphalt, excited, running around and not particularly looking very scared. I wondered why they did not share my fear. How strange, I thought.

3

The ground was shaking back and forth from aftershocks. I lost my balance several times and had to crouch on the ground to remain upright. This was my first earthquake. I fought back nausea for a few minutes and thought I would faint.

After the initial quake, most of the teachers and support staff left campus and headed out to retrieve their own children. (These departures occurred throughout California and later prompted a Senate bill that now requires all teachers to serve as public safety workers for 48 hours after a disaster). I found myself standing on the blacktop wondering what to do next.

In the Trenches

In the distance, I saw Nancy (my principal) walking across the playground carrying a pile of bullhorns over her shoulder. She seemed to be headed in my direction, pointing her finger and yelling at students who crossed her path. As soon as she spotted me, she walked over to where I was standing.

"I know you're scared," she said, as she tried to comfort me. "I can see it in your eyes. You are an intelligent woman, so it won't take you long to process this earthquake." She began to educate me on the spot. "Are you aware that very few people die from earthquakes or are injured after the initial quake? We'll get a few more aftershocks, but don't worry, they won't be as strong as the first earthquake. I need your help," she continued, holding out one of the smaller bullhorns. "Do you think you can calm the children and do something to get our parents under control?"

Stunned and still reeling from the quake, something must have come over me, as I reached out and grabbed one of her bullhorns. Nancy smiled and pointed to a group of students punching one another near the fence. "There's your first assignment," she said, darting off in the other direction.

The remainder of the day, I mobilized student groups to wait in safe harbor areas, while I appointed instructional assistants to supervisory roles. I checked classrooms for injured or frightened students and calmed kindergartners sitting on the asphalt, crying for their mothers. I teamed up with the library clerk to launch a student pick up center. Parents had begun to storm the front office, and some had climbed locked gates and demanded to see their children. I wished I had not worn high heels and mentally registered a note to pack sneakers for the next emergency. It was a very long day on the clock, but each hour seemed to go by in an instant.

After all students were accounted for and sent home for the day, I reported to Nancy's office for a debriefing. I was exhausted, covered in dust, and felt a bit odd. I remember thinking that I had done well in this emergency situation. During the debriefing, Nancy confirmed my beliefs. As I look back on that day, the day of the infamous Long Beach earthquake, I became keenly aware that I possessed leadership skills and liked being in charge.

Live and Learn

The following day, we all went back to teaching and followed our normal school day routines. Around midmorning, Nancy came into my classroom, walked right up to the blackboard where I was teaching and informed me that I needed to get into an administration program. "I couldn't have managed yesterday without your help," she said. "You have the potential to become a school principal. Do it—we need people like you in leadership."

In all my years of teaching, no one had ever suggested I become a school administrator. In my experience, the school administrators I knew were mostly men and former coaches or physical education teachers. I knew I would have to go back to grad school for another California credential that would take a lot of time. Moreover, I knew that administrators worked longer hours. Teaching, while difficult, sure looked easier to me than being an administrator.

Over the next few weeks, however, I continued to reflect on the day of the earthquake, a day of being in charge. It was no secret to my friends that I was looking for a challenge. I speculated that this desire was most likely a response to the confidence gained from moving to California and working in a new and exciting environment.

As a result of Nancy's encouragement, I enrolled in California State University Long Beach and registered for the initial credential course in their educational administration program.

Back to School Night

I can recall the first day of graduate school, as if it were yesterday. About thirty students waited patiently for our professor to arrive. It was our first course in educational administration, and the room was filled with nervous energy. Dr. Williams, a rather large, stately woman, made her presence and began to apprise us how class would function. She belted out the semester's requirements, as if she'd just completed a duty tour in the marines—six research papers, seven textbooks, a group project, two individual presentations and concluded her list with a midterm and final.

Her speech went on for what seemed like thirty minutes, and then all of a sudden she paused in mid-sentence, as if to collect her thoughts. She rose from her chair, walked over to the front row of students, peered over her glasses and then pronounced, "For those of you who won't be able to put in the required time for this class, make no mistake, you've got no business wanting to be an administrator. If that's your story, I advise you to get up and leave this class right now."

Wow, what bad luck. My first class, and I drew turbo instructor. What were the chances, I thought? All of a sudden, I heard a peculiar snapping sound resonate from the woman sitting behind me. It sounded like a brief case being closed. Then, I heard more snapping sounds coming from different directions. One person, an older gentleman, made the first gesture. He rose from his seat and snarled, "I don't need this crap," and literally stormed out of the room. Ten others immediately followed his lead. The room was silent. When the dust settled, there were ten of us left. The professor, acting as if nothing had happened, continued her lecture, giving directions on the various assignments for the remaining two hours.

When I returned home, I shared the story with my husband. "Why didn't you get up and leave?" he asked.

"I was too scared to move," I replied. "My legs were shaking. Believe me, if I could have, I would have."

The following week, the class returned to its original size. I imagined the "university people" had a talk with Dr. Williams and directed her to call back the students. The class became a wonderful learning experience, and once again I was enjoying another adventure in a new arena—educational administration. During my two years in the program, I learned about finance, personnel, law, governance, instruction, and my personal favorite, leadership. I treasured every minute of it. I was back in my element, experiencing new things and thriving.

Stumbling Block

My excitement about becoming a school administrator ended abruptly. I had enrolled in a two-year program and was eager to complete the credential requirements and begin work as an assistant principal, as soon as possible. I queried my colleagues, "How does this work? Are there a lot of administrative jobs available?"

Disillusionment ensued, as people cautioned that world of educational administration was plagued with competition and disappointment. My quest to find a job, they warned, would be fraught with obstacles and frustration. Everyone surveyed reported, "Administration jobs are hard to get." I began to hate myself for being so naïve. I was under the assumption that the process for securing an administrative position would be similar to getting a teaching job in Syracuse or the position that came so easily in California. Nothing could have been further from the truth.

The Game Plan

My husband and I decided we needed a plan. After all, we agreed, our good planning got us across the county—how hard could this be? We decided (notice I said "we") that I would apply to any assistant principal opening, commutable within one hour. We placed a Los Angeles map on the carpet, fixed a piece of string on Seal Beach, California and drew a 360 degree circle (approximately 40 miles) around the pinpoint. There it was, clear as the circle drawn on the map. I would apply to any district within that range. Our plan, which I later termed the "360 Plan," is a template I've used and recommended to others for many years.

The second part of the plan involved making a chart containing rows devoted to each district; dates of applications, interview schedules, etc. By late February, fifteen school districts were entered on the chart, all in receipt of my paperwork. By the end of March, fourteen sent notifications, essentially saying, "Thanks, but no thanks," in their rejection letters.

I shared my distress with Nancy, and she asked to see my paperwork. After a quick review, she wasted no time in saying, "Your paperwork needs work. Your resume is horrible. You've listed *teacher* accomplishments. Don't get me wrong," she encouraged, "your accomplishments are good, but you need to pull them forward, in order to make them sound like *leadership* accomplishments. You aren't applying for a teacher position, you know." She was tough. "Go buy a book on resumes, and redo this. A better resume will get you in the door."

In late April, I had a new resume and my "list" of potential jobs approached twenty. I color coded each category (an old teaching habit). For example, red meant no interview, and blue indicated the district had received my paperwork. As a personal motivator, I hung the chart on the kitchen wall and strategized daily.

Nothing Ventured, Nothing Gained

It was good news when Santa Ana Unified contacted me to interview for an assistant principal position (thank you Nancy). I spent the weekend at South Coast Plaza purchasing a new suit, shoes, and jewelry. The interview was scheduled for a Monday, which gave me all day Sunday to think about the interview. While somewhat anxious, I wasn't particularly worried about the interview. I was an excellent teacher, had obtained all As in grad school, and had confidence going into the interview.

I arrived early for the interview and was greeted by a very young man. Without time to check my hair or use the restroom, he motioned for me to follow him into a small conference room. As I entered the room, I saw what seemed like fifteen to twenty people sitting around a table. The claustrophobic visual still haunts me to this day—very small space, stuffy, stagnant air, heads, heads and more heads, peering up from notebooks. Not a good experience.

The interview panel wasted no time in shelling out a magnitude of questions: "Why do you want to work for us? What skills do you have to lead a school? How will you implement a discipline program for junior high students, and what will you do for our English Language Learners? What makes a good teacher? How do you make decisions?"

I froze, caught like a deer in headlights. In retrospect, given more time to think about these questions, I probably could have answered most of them. But, unfortunately I'd never prepared responses in advance about these issues and couldn't answer many of the questions. "I must have looked quite unprepared," I thought. "I need to get out of here!"

The interview lasted less than ten minutes. If memory serves me right, I think some of the people sitting around the table were beginning to feel sorry for me. As I got up to leave the room, many of the panel members looked away. The young fellow, obviously the lead interviewer, led me out of the room and said with some degree of reassurance, "Don't worry, you did fine. We'll let you know."

"Yeah, let me know alright," I thought. "Let me know how ridiculous I sounded." I couldn't wait to get out of the building. As I drove home. I became angrier and angrier at myself for not preparing properly for the interview. "All this work to get an administrative credential, and I fall down in the interview. What a waste of time."

Hunkering Down

Thoughts of giving up only lasted a few days. As a teenager, my swimming coach had a saying, "Go strong or don't go at all." His inspirational quote gave me comfort, and I started to equate looking for a new job much like preparing for a swimming marathon. As a result of my new perspective, I practiced interviewing by making up potential questions that a district might ask an assistant principal applicant. I knew my greatest strengths and accomplishments, could articulate school discipline procedures, and could respond intelligently to possible finance questions. My opening statement had been committed to memory, and I was able to share my goals for becoming an administrator. I even had an engaging response to the question, "Why should we hire you?"

Great news—I received a second chance. Ontario-Montclair, a large desert district within my sixty mile radius, invited me for an interview. They informed me I would be one of fifteen people being interviewed for two assistant principal positions. I was thrilled.

I can remember this interview and arriving at the district office parking lot as if it were yesterday (these defining moments take root). Ontario's temperature had soared to 105 degrees, and as I walked across the parking lot, I could feel the soles of my shoes catching fire from the burning asphalt. The most vivid memory, however, was my shear amazement at how I could work up a sweat in less than twenty seconds, walking from the car to the district office main entrance. I was beginning to think we'd made an error in calculations, when this desert town appeared on my 360 degree interview map. "Not to worry," I cautioned myself, "this heat won't distract me from my mission to do well. I'm prepared. I'm ready for this interview—and I'm going in strong."

At the conclusion of the interview, I was quite pleased with my performance. I knew the panel could sense my confidence and how prepared I was. My answers just rolled out. Something nagged at me, however, as I left the building. The interview was completed in less than fifteen minutes. As a self-protection measure, I put these thoughts out of my mind and began to dream about my first day on the job, what Nancy would think about the promotion, and how I would celebrate. I didn't want anything to interfere with my optimistic view about my performance. The drive from Ontario to Seal Beach took about an hour, allowing plenty of time to reflect. I couldn't think of anything I would have done differently in the interview.

Arriving back at Seal Beach, I could hear the phone ringing, as I walked into the house. As soon as I answered, I recognized the Ontario Montclair superintendent's voice on the other end. Excited and impressed, I speculated.... "Superintendents don't call losers."

It didn't take him long to say, "You did a good job, but unfortunately we've gone with two other candidates."

"What did I do wrong?" I queried, holding back my disappointment. The superintendent was a real nice man in the interview and again on the phone. I thought I'd risk his approachable manner to take this opportunity and push him for some information about the interview.

"Nothing, really," he said. "But if you're open to criticism, I'd like to give you some advice. You sounded somewhat like a "know it all" in the interview. I personally liked what you had to say, but the panel thought you were a bit too rigid. Loosen up, and let people see who you really are. Showcase your talents and how well you relate to people and students."

I thanked him for the advice, hung up, took off my suit, threw myself on the bed, and began to cry. "How the heck am I going to make this happen?" I said. "This is no swimming meet—this is hell."

Scoring the Goal!

Over the next few months, I worked hard to plan and package my skills, as I continued to interview for jobs. My husband grilled me on interview questions and offered critical commentary to improve my delivery. By mid-June, I was getting worried. The window of opportunity for getting a job as an assistant principal was closing. Three districts remained on my list but had not called me for an interview. I had not heard back from them, which I perceived was a positive sign.

Just before the Fourth of July holiday, Torrance Unified called to say I had been selected to interview. The district had two assistant principal openings, and the woman on the phone asked if I was still interested. "Still interested," I laughed to myself and thought, "when can I start?"

I arrived at the interview twenty minutes before the scheduled appointment and sat in the car, reviewing my notes. I was confident I could answer any question. My challenge now was to act self-assured, and show poise in the interview. I walked into the district office and located the women's room for an opportunity to check my hair and makeup. I smiled at myself in the mirror and told myself, "Go strong."

The interview was a positive experience. Upon entering the conference room, one woman complimented my suit; another remarked that she liked my shoes. The panel members were very cordial, and everyone in the room was smiling or nodding their heads in approval, as I answered question after question. I could feel a connection forming between myself and the panel and was getting excited about the prospect of working for these people.

Two questions took an interesting slant during the interview. The lead interviewer—the assistant superintendent of personnel—asked two pointed questions, which went something like this: "We have two openings, Marilou. We have an assistant principal opening for a middle school and another position that will cover two elementary schools. If offered a job in our district, which one would you prefer?"

I had never been asked a question like this before and was getting encouraged. In my mind, two variables surfaced relative to the question. First, the middle school assignment was what I really wanted and secondly, the elementary assistant principal position, while still a job, involved working between two schools and was not a particularly plum assignment.

I knew I wanted "a job" and would take either opportunity if offered, so I responded by saying, "I would love to work in your district as an administrator. This question, however, leaves me a bit 'caught in the middle,' since I love working with middle school children and have secondary experience. I also have over eight years of elementary experience, so I would have to say, either position would be a natural fit for my experience and skills. The lead interviewer smiled and responded that he had just finished reading the new state middle school reform document entitled, *Caught in the Middle* and remarked that he liked my response.

The second question caught me off guard, as I had not planned for this question in advance. The lead interviewer pulled out my resume and waved it around the table as he asked, "Do you have any skeletons in your closet that we should know about before making a decision?"

My head was spinning. "What were they looking for?" I wondered. As I thought about what I was going to say, I ransacked my mind to think of anything that could be considered a "skeleton." Surely they were not thinking I had been demoted, fired, or arrested for a crime?

Skeletons in my closet? I said, "No, I live a clean life, have done well in all my jobs, and have only positive things going on in my career. The only thing in my closet that I can think of that could be considered a skeleton, in my husband's opinion, would be a whole lot of new shoes." They roared with laughter. I was quite pleased with myself, as I mentally planned my celebration for landing this job.

At the conclusion of the interview, the lead walked me out to my car and informed me he would be calling finalists by the end of the week. I was thrilled when he called the next day to offer me the middle school assistant principal position and asked when I could start work. I was excited, relieved, and proud of myself. As a result of my focus on planning and perfecting my paperwork, combined with vigorous interview preparation, I was able to reach my ultimate goal; that of attaining a job in educational leadership. All of my hard work and determination had finally paid off.

While I had a mentor who encouraged me to take the leap from teaching to administration, I did not have the privilege to work with anyone in the field to help me prepare for an interview. Mentors or coaches for educators are now a common phenomenon, but when I attempted to cross over from teaching to administration over twenty years ago, these support systems were virtually non-existent. I know that if I had been afforded an opportunity to work with a close mentor or had the chance to read a book like this one, I would have reached my goal sooner, with less stress.

As you have learned from my story, the path one chooses in life may not always be an easy one. I am reminded of an anonymous quote that says, "In order to succeed you must first be willing to fail." No kidding. Through simple acts of failure and disappointment, I learned a lot about my aspirations to become a leader and what it actually took to make them a reality.

I was fortunate to have had the opportunity to move across the country with my husband. As a woman who had little confidence to handle major life changes, I look back and value every second of the experience. Seeing different places and meeting new people enabled me to change my thoughts and attitude, which ultimately changed my world. I was also privileged to cross paths with a female administrator, who encouraged me to take on a leadership role in education.

After submitting over twenty applications and interviewing for five school districts, I proudly accepted the offer to serve as the middle school assistant principal for Torrance Unified School District. Success at last!

Why You Should Read This Book

If you took the time to order this book and have read this far, you are motivated to land a new promotion in your career. If someone bought this book for you, they obviously think you have the potential to move up in your career. Very few people, in my experience, gain a new job easily. Those that gain a job on their first attempt may be one of the "chosen few," groomed for the job within their own districts. A few other applicants have what we call a "Tom Cruise" charisma that can totally impress an interview panel. You and I, however—the remaining ninety-nine percent of applicants—must struggle and work hard to win a promotion. I only wish I had been able to read the strategies suggested in this book early on in my career.

This book is the outcome of my work in education, professional consulting work, and mentoring others to the next level in their careers. I wrote this book to help others gain traction in their job searches. I know what it feels like to want to advance in one's career. I also know how disappointment can cripple one's motivation and spirit during the rejection process. It hurts.

This book can't ease the pain of rejection but will make the journey to your goals a lot easier. I have served on interview panels and have seen the range of candidates, from the very best to the very worst, and am amazed at the lack of preparation some educators exhibit when they put their lives on line at the interview table. The knowledge and recommendations you will read in this book will add depth to your understanding of the requirements for a leadership position.

Rules of the Game

This book defines successful tactics to leverage your talents, knowledge, and abilities and bring them forward in a job application strategy, to win a new job in educational leadership. Most importantly, it shares "Insider Tips" that will help you maintain a "go strong attitude" within four winning areas: *Planning, Packaging, Preparing* and *Persevering*.

Restated for those who like the research approach, the "Rules of the Game" suggests one has the capacity to understand and manage variables in the hiring process, that have promotional influence. Specifically, these rules are divided into four areas, detailed in this simple branch model:

1. The capacity to plan one's career path.
2. The capacity to package and manage one's paperwork and branding.
3. The capacity to prepare and excel at the interview process.

4. The capacity to persevere in spite of the many obstacles encountered during the hiring process.

Planning - The Game Plan

Strategies to plan for your next move are shared, along with how to ask for recommendations and references from key people in past job assignments.

Four different pathways are explored in Career Bridges: (1) teacher to assistant principal; (2) assistant principal to principal; (3) principal to district office; and finally (4) district office to superintendent.

As a long time educator, I have crossed over to each career level, and I am certain that they all required special moves. Also, in this section, timing issues, such as when to announce you're looking for a new position or how to tell your boss you're moving on are addressed, with proven strategies to navigate these unfamiliar and sometimes "dangerous" waters.

Packaging - the Art of Self-Promotion

This topic is easy. You can't get the job, if you can't get to the interview table. I recall, as a successful, seasoned middle school principal, armed with a doctorate and flying applications for an assistant superintendent position thinking, "Hire me now—I'm good, I'm a winner, and I'm ready to become an assistant superintendent. What more do I need?"

Wrong. Interviews were almost nonexistent. After refining my resume to integrate school accomplishments to fit with district administration goals, I finally started to receive interviews. This section discusses the initial application process, letters of introduction, killer resumes, and timing issues related to moving on. Remember, you may be good at what you do and have what it takes to move on—but if you don't package your paperwork to express those qualities and accomplishments, no one will invite you for an interview. No interview equals no job promotion.

Preparation – Practice Makes Perfect

What a pity to finally get to the interview table and then end up looking naïve. How misguided it is of us to think we don't need to prepare fully for one of the most high stakes moments in our career, where "a panel of experts" will assess how we walk in the door, place a value judgment on what we look like, evaluate our every sentence, and then finally turn to one another and ask, "Do we like this person?"

This section details key points to help you succeed in an interview and prepare for this critical opportunity. Key strands from predictable questions are explored with commentary and notes for review. The reader is encouraged to commit these strands to memory and internalize them, so they can be used with ease in an interview. Finally, a plan is presented to help you succeed, once promoted and on the job.

Perseverance – Approaching the Finish Line

Again, I am reminded of an anonymous quote that says, "Persistence prevails when all else fails." This chapter sheds light on how to stay the course, when the going gets tough. You can plan, package, and prepare ad infinitum, but if you lack the perseverance to charge on when new hurdles are presented, you may not accomplish your goals. For that reason, this chapter aims to mobilize your tenacity, by offering encouragement and strong advice. Real time, real people tips and inspirations are included from those in the field who have walked in your shoes and succeeded, in spite of the obstacles.

Scoring the Goal

The formula is quite simple. Working within four key focus areas, an educator can leverage specific winning game strategies to move on to the next level in their career. It's a simple winning formula:

1. Good planning = Getting on the scoreboard.
2. Precision packaging = Scoring points.
3. Intense interview prep = Score takes off and soars.
4. Determination and perseverance = A goal is scored!

When all four areas are synchronized with one another, the potential for winning success is unlimited.

Parting Shots

At this point, you are no doubt contemplating becoming a school administrator or looking for advancement in your administrative position. There are thousands of books written to help people excel at and/or keep their job, once promoted. There are few books, if any, on the shelves today that focus on advancing one's career in educational administration. This book aims to make your special journey a little easier, by offering some effective tools and "Insider Tips."

Start your plan, use what you can, begin packaging yourself—and prepare, prepare, prepare. If you successfully leverage the winning game strategies in this book, you will maximize your chances to move ahead in your career and score your goal.

If you tear a page out to post on your wall, put a sticky note on a page or highlight passages in this book—I've done my job. Consider this publication a "rule book" to define and improve upon your job seeking skills. Most of all, go strong and energize yourself to go the distance and cross the finish line. While the journey may be long and hard, I can assure you there is nothing more rewarding as an educational leader than to be able to make a difference for children and young adults.

Now let's get to work and make it happen!

Section I:

THE SCORE CARD

Moving up to the next level in your career is not an easy task, and you need to be ready. Before you set out on your path, take this short quiz below that asks a few personal and professional questions.

1. Are you being granted interviews after applying for advanced positions of leadership?

2. Does your cover letter and resume stand out in the crowd and show paper screeners you're ready for the job?

3. Are you aware of the wide range of questions asked in interviews?

4. Are you prepared for the challenges of the high stakes interview environment?

5. Are you tired of coming in "second?"

6. Do you have a professional mentor?

7. Do you know how to inform your immediate supervisors about your plans to move up?

8. Do you know how to ask for stellar recommendations from key people?

9. Do you know how to accept an offer of employment?

10. Do you know what to do (announcements, resignations, etc.) once offered a new position?

11. Do you know how to negotiate salary or an employment contract?

12. Are you prepared to make mistakes and learn from them?

13. Do you have the time needed to prepare for and deliver a stellar interview?

14. Do you have the resiliency to withstand rejection and keep applying for the positions you want?

If any of these questions resonant with you in some manner, continue on to the "Answer Key" below to check your readiness.

1. Are you being granted interviews when applying for advanced positions of leadership?

Most rookies to the game underestimate the importance of one important detail—if you can't get to the interview, you obviously can't get hired.

Gaining an interview may be the single most important event for securing a new job promotion. The process involves packaging your written materials to get your foot in the door. Part of that packaging includes obtaining recommendation letters, writing a killer resume and having an ongoing successful career path. Many factors contribute to gaining an interview, and we'll discuss them thoroughly in this book.

As a superintendent, many resumes that crossed my desk were frequently bulleted with job specifications, rather than accomplishments. Interview screening members all know the job qualifications for a principal. An applicant may state on a resume that they oversee thirty teachers. What a paper screener wants to see, however, is what you accomplished with these teachers that makes you stand out above the rest of the applicants. A lack of stated accomplishments on a resume is one of the most prevalent application errors seen in our field of education.

A resume takes time to build and should always be considered a "work in progress." When I applied for a superintendent position, I used my original resume template created when I applied for assistant principal positions. I kept my resume at work and continually updated my accomplishments and added new details. Of course, with each new job, I redesigned my resume to suit particular job specifications, but the ground work had already been done.

2. Does your cover letter and resume stand out in the crowd and show paper screeners you're ready for the job?

The cover letter and the resume are the primary keys to gaining an interview. If you apply for a position of leadership, you obviously think you have what it takes to do the job. What does your paperwork say about you? Can it be read with clarity?

Will a sixty-year-old paper screener, perhaps the assistant superintendent from human resources, be able to read the font size, or does he have to work hard to make out the words?

Do you make it easy for screeners to notice your qualifications and warrant a "must see" at the interview level?

Have you done some amazing work for students, saved the district money, increased student attendance, lowered discipline referrals, raised test scores, created a program that makes teaching more effective, or developed a new plan that everyone raves about?

If so, begin compiling a list of your accomplishments. You should have six to eight activities for each position held. You can fine-tune your resume, after reading specific tips in the "Packaging: The Art of Self Promotion" chapter included later in the book.

3. Are you aware of the wide range of questions asked in interviews?

Every job interview begins with the question, "Well Pete, thank you for being here today to spend some time with us, so we can all get to know you better. Could you please take a few minutes and tell us why you believe your skills are a match for this position and/or why you want this position?" In other words… "Why are you here?"

If you don't answer this one effectively, the interview is essentially over.

I recall one candidate responding to the opening question, rambling on about everything imaginable for over twenty minutes. I felt sorry for him and wished I could signal him to "cool it" and move on to the next question. The superintendent observing the interview had no mercy. He stood up while the man was still talking and left the room. As the interview went on, I wondered if this applicant was aware of the implications of the superintendent exiting the interview and if he knew how much help he needed with his interviewing skills.

In the field of educational administration, as elsewhere, applicants often "don't know what they don't know." To assist with areas that need to be addressed, I have provided what I call "Scrimmage Notes." We'll cover them later on in the important chapter entitled, "Preparation: Practice Makes Perfect."

4. Are you prepared for the challenges of the high stakes interview environment?

An applicant must prepare notes and practice, before attending this important one-shot opportunity. You don't get a second chance. You can't say, "Oh sorry, do you mind if I come back in and start over?"

I have hired many administrators throughout my career. I learned that applicants who succeed in gaining new jobs have a few things in common. Winning candidates are confident in the interview. They walk into the interview room at ease, with a smile on their face, shaking everyone's hand. They gracefully accept any water offered, take a seat, sit back with their hands folded and smile. They are dressed for the occasion—often in a navy blue suit—and if female, have no signs of distracting jewelry, perfume, strange hair or makeup. Successful job candidates share an opening joke, story, or something to ease their nervous energy; something simple like how nice the drive was on the way to the interview.

Occasionally, the lead interviewer will say, "Take the hot seat, young man." Everyone laughs. Some candidates are good on the comeback. "Looks like it's my turn on American Idol."

After the first question is asked, or if the timing is right, the candidate takes a quick moment to thank everyone in the room for the opportunity to interview. Nothing special or over the top, just a quick statement to add, "Before we begin, I would like to take this opportunity to say thank you for giving me the opportunity to interview." That's it. Short and simple.

Then the interview begins. The easy questions are usually first, progressing to the more difficult ones, as the interview gains momentum. Sometimes one person asks all the questions; sometimes

21

everyone on the panel will have a chance to ask a question. The winning candidate should always make eye contact with the questioner, as he or she answers the question in less than two or three minutes, and no longer. Answers should be knowledgeable and include personal experiences and examples. Stellar candidates leverage their experiences and skills within each question, to show how they can contribute their talents to the new district.

Those who make it to the finals are the ones who have given examples of good work or programs they have personally developed. Winning candidates often find just the right question to share a heartwarming story, proving to the panel, "I have heart. I have integrity. I have the skills to implement my knowledge—hire me!"

Outstanding candidates know how to weave their personal touch throughout the interview. They might share a story about helping a student who has gone astray, talk about why they chose education, or share their version about coming to America as an isolated and frightened non-English student. People respond to sincere and heartfelt moments in interviews, and a judicially applied dose of emotion can take a candidate over the finish line.

A story of caution regarding emotion. I once served on a panel in which a candidate was interviewing for a high school principal position. He was well-known throughout the district as an excellent administrator, and the position had his name on it. Midway through the interview, the candidate shared that his father had recently passed away and how he had developed courage and resolution from the experience. In telling the story, he choked up and lowered his head for what seemed like an eternity. When he looked up, it was obvious he had been crying. He gained his composure within a few seconds, but it was too late. The district was looking for a strong leader and for them, crying in an interview was not acceptable. As a result, this talented applicant lost out on a position that could have easily been his.

Forgetting to mention students can also ruin an otherwise good interview. I worked with a superintendent search consultant on a project and admired her skills. She was wise and had learned much from her years of experience in the field. We were talking one day about superintendent searches in general and about what types of candidates make it to the superintendency. She shared that, in her experience overseeing hundreds of superintendent interviews, only one in five candidates ever makes a comment about students. "They get overly technical in the interview and forget why they came into education," she declared. "When candidates forget to talk about our main product—the children—an interview panel loses interest. This is a *people*, a *child-centered* business. They should tell us they love kids and want to make a difference for them."

5. Are you tired of coming in second?

Coming in second doesn't get you the job—but it's still good, right? No. Coming in second is agonizing, excruciating, and just plain hurts. No matter how you slice it, coming in second is painful and worse than not making the finals. So close... yet so far away.

I'd like you to take a guess here. Do you know how long it takes prospective superintendent candidates to land their first superintendent position? Approximately six interviews! The number of interviews climbs even higher to obtain the second superintendency. On average, an assistant principal can expect to interview at least five times, before gaining a principal position.

Second place is not a "bad" place to be. It is unfortunate, however, when a candidate continues to accept the loss and do nothing to increase their chances of success. Second placers have to work harder. They must believe in themselves and not take the loss personally. They must get back in the game and try again and believe defeat is not an option. They must learn that, in order to make improvements, they need to determine why they came in second.

Sometimes a search consultant or personnel director will meet with a candidate to review the interview. On one occasion, I called the assistant superintendent of human resources, after interviewing for an assistant superintendent position. I asked if he would offer commentary in a face-to-face meeting to discuss my interview. He agreed and spent some time with me to review my answers.

"You did a great job in the interview," he exclaimed. "The panel loved you. One thing, however, I'd like to mention. Two times in the interview you indicated you wanted to be a superintendent. This was an interview for an *assistant* superintendent. This put the panel off somewhat. They didn't want to hear about you wanting to become a superintendent."

I had assumed most districts would be encouraged when hearing that their applicant was interested in advancing within their ranks and would demonstrate desire to work hard for the district. I was wrong. They were only interested in filling the job at hand. See how easy that was?

On my next interview, I left the superintendent part out and was promoted to assistant superintendent of educational services. While my long-term goal involved being a superintendent, I learned to focus on the job at hand and not distract the interview panel.

If you continue to come in second, try to find out if there were any speed bumps in your last interview. Many district administrators in charge of an interview will share something that can help you improve, since they have walked in your shoes. If you can't gain access to that information, sit down and take a hard look at your performance and ask yourself what it would take to bring your interviewing skills to a "10."

One habit I often used after an interview or high stakes presentation to gain perspective of how well I performed was to have a trusted person rate me. I would ask a good colleague, or in the case of an interview, a search consultant, the following: "On a scale from 1 to 10, with 10 being the best, how would you rate my performance today?" In many cases, they would award an 8 or 9. The next question became: "What would it take on my part to make it a 10?" Try this strategy the next time you give a speech, deliver a PowerPoint, or participate in an interview.

6. Do you have a professional mentor?

When taking on the challenge to move ahead in your career, it's important to work with a mentor with skills in the interview process. Reading this book will provide much needed groundwork, but having a mentor to answer your questions about a particular district or to review your resume and provide constructive feedback is invaluable.

Many of my colleagues have shared that they were hesitant to approach me for career advice, because of my busy schedule as a superintendent. Quite frankly, many thought they would be a burden. What they didn't know was that, for me personally, it was almost impossible to turn them down.

Don't be afraid to take a chance and ask someone you trust to serve as your mentor, during this time of critical need. Most of us remember the hurdles we jumped through to gain our current jobs, and many of us are enthusiastic about helping our colleagues. But again, you can't get help, if you don't ask. Although asking for help is hard for some of us, it may be the most important step you will take on your journey to your next promotion.

7. Do you know how to inform your immediate supervisors about your plans to move up?

There is nothing worse than to meet your boss at the copy machine and remark, "Hey, I just got a call from Dr. Tellall at California School District. He asked me if they should hire you. What's up with this?" While this faux pas is not a career killer, it can make for some hard feelings generated by your current employer.

Negotiating this political mine field requires skill and courage. If you are seeking another job or have already submitted paperwork to a new district, learn how to approach this dilemma in the "Planning: Developing the Game Plan" chapter.

8. Do you know how to ask for stellar recommendations from key people?

It's fairly easy to ask someone for a recommendation, but another thing altogether to have them write one that stands out over all the others. Most districts require three or four current recommendations from your supervisors. Whenever I served as a paper screener, I was made responsible for checking letters of recommendations. Major flaws I found included undated letters, too many letters written by the applicant's subordinates (glowing reports about how much they love the boss) and outdated letters. Unfortunately, these applications were usually sent to the circular file.

9. Do you know how to accept an offer of employment?

Finally, the phone call arrives and the person on the other end exclaims, "We were impressed with you and want to know when you can start." This is fantastic news—but don't throw a party just yet, there's a lot of work to do. Navigating this political road is a lot like balancing on a tight rope.

I recall a former colleague, who accepted a position as an assistant superintendent in a neighboring district. She was well-liked in her own school district and wanted to "help them out," so she submitted her letter of resignation before her official appointment to the new district. You might guess how this story ends. The new district changed their decision in midstream on the position, and my friend was now in the throes of a career dilemma. Fortunately, her former district chose to take her back, but this could have been avoided, if she had followed some simple protocols, which are discussed later on in this book.

10. Do you know what to do (announcements, resignations, etc.) once offered a new position?

Your superintendent or boss will be upset, if they hear you have been offered another job from anyone else but you. Their discontent can shift to cardiac arrest, if you happen to be held in high esteem by any board members. Advance notification and planning can produce a positive exit strategy that will keep people talking well about you for years to come, even though they may be angry you are leaving them.

Strategies to overcome this issue include sending out press releases and/or composing a letter in advance to be disseminated to staff immediately after your announcement to leave. As superintendent, I rarely got angry, but one memorable exception included discovering from a board member that my assistant superintendent accepted a job with a nonprofit organization. Another involved a phone call asking about the qualifications of another assistant superintendent, who had applied for a job in another district. On both occasions, I shared my discontent and disappointment with both cabinet members. If you are a professional—act like one, and tell your boss you're looking. In addition, your new boss will not look highly on any attempts to keep your former boss in the dark.

11. Do you know how to negotiate salary or an employment contract?

Employment contracts are usually standard for superintendents, as well as some assistant superintendents. Some candidates are so excited to finally be selected that they neglect to read the "fine print" in the contracts they are asked to sign. "Not to worry," the district representative advises. "This is a boilerplate contract that's been used for years in this district. The sooner we get this taken care of, the sooner you can be approved by the board."

There are many horror stories circulating in our industry related to this issue. I have personally known superintendents who signed one-year contracts (standard is three), and others who signed agreements stating they could be demoted to a lower position, if the board was not satisfied with their performance. One superintendent even agreed to a contract that stipulated he could not take a single vacation day, without advanced board approval.

While there are many reputable resources and people who can help you with contract negotiations, some simple tips to get you started and provide some areas of caution are covered in the chapter dealing with preparation.

12. Are you prepared to make mistakes and learn from them?

Sounds like one giant platitude, right?

We have been taught that those who gain success and happiness must be willing to learn from their mistakes. It's true. You will make mistakes as you apply for positions of advancement, and you must learn from them. More importantly, however, if you don't take the time to reflect upon what you did wrong, you are bound to repeat the same mistake, thus lowering your chances to achieve your goals.

As shared earlier in this book, my naivety when responding to questions during my first administration interview still makes me cringe. I don't like to think about how uninformed I was. By facing my own embarrassment, I was able to reflect on my performance and become stronger in the next interview. Do not let failures cripple you.

Keep in mind, throughout your journey, that failures come with the territory. School administrators have a very rewarding, prestigious, and powerful role to play in education. With judicially applied power, they are able to put their talents to work and make a difference for students. Failures are often a byproduct of the job. Resiliency and the ability to examine and grow from one's mistakes is the most critical component for experiencing overall success on the job.

13. Do you have the time needed to prepare for and deliver a stellar interview?

You can't win in an interview for a top position of leadership, without preparing in advance. It just doesn't happen. If you plan to shine in an interview, you must answer key questions, be at the top of your form, sound smart, be sociable, and look like you know what you're doing—and this all takes deliberate preparation. You must be willing to put in the time to fully prepare for an interview.

I mentored a principal who wanted to become an assistant superintendent. Before each interview, he would spend time on the district's website to learn about the district's goals and test scores. When I interviewed for a superintendent position, I would call the county office and request a copy of the district's budget. I would spend an afternoon charting ideas gleaned from the budget that I hoped to share in the interview.

A colleague put very aptly, "I've interviewed for five different districts and each time spent hours researching their test scores, strategic plans, technology, and instructional action plans. I believe the new knowledge gained in the process of preparing for all these interviews actually led to getting my current job."

14. Do you have the resiliency to withstand rejection and keep applying for the positions you want?

As an executive mentoring consultant, I work with many candidates who apply and interview over a long period of time. When they are on top of their interview game, some will tell me they want to stop interviewing. "I've had it with rejection," one candidate exclaims. "My family can't take this anymore. I must not be made for this work, if I keep losing out." Having a career coach or critical friend who can guide you through this dark tunnel is very important. It is very difficult to take on this project alone, so when you feel like giving up, it helps to have a mentor to call.

Many applicants are reluctant to share any defeat, because they think it will make them look bad in their own districts and worry their colleagues or bosses will start doubting their abilities. One superintendent applied five times in an attempt to make a lateral move to a larger district with more growth opportunity "My board is beginning to think they have a loser on board," he said. "They are beginning to believe that if other districts don't want me, why should they? I'm walking a fine line here."

Research suggests it takes applicants about five interviews to make a "lateral" move, and find a match that aligns with one's talents and personality. The rewards for success will outweigh the risks you need to take. The journey will be a challenge, but do not give up in your attempt to move your career along or seek a new growth opportunity.

Parting Shots

Every author will make necessary assumptions about his or her audience when writing a book. When writing this book, I made the following assumptions:

- You are ambitious and competitive.
- You are a high performer in your field.
- You are considering career advancement.
- You have colleagues in the field but do not have a designated mentor.
- You are working on a resume and cover letter, but want to refine them.
- You will do what it takes to attain your goals.

Do any of the above bullets strike a chord? If so, get out your yellow highlighter and sticky notes—and let's get to work on this project!

Section II:

PLANNING - Developing the Game Plan

"By failing to plan, you are planning to fail."
~ Benjamin Franklin

If you have ever spent time working as a classroom teacher, you can probably recall your daily lesson plans made to survive past ten in the morning. I'm sure that's why God invented planbooks for educators, as he watched teachers trying to manage the chaos without one. This same maxim holds true for finding a job. Without a focused, well thought out plan, trying to move up in educational administration can be as frustrating as having no planbook, surrounded by thirty-five needy students in a classroom.

The wise quote, "Fail to plan, plan to fail" reminds us of the importance of setting goals, strategies to achieve those goals, and action steps to get things done. As educators, we are constantly planning our next event, meeting, project, or academic achievement. We almost do this without thinking. Successful educators understand how good planning helps them deal with the unexpected that inevitably occurs. (Superintendent Planner, Corwin 2009).

Some people decide to become administrators overnight, without much thought or planning. They comb through job openings and fill out application forms, with the dream of moving on and picking up a bigger paycheck. These applicants often end up frustrated or embarrassed, as they find themselves unprepared to deal with questions asked in high stakes interviews. You may choose to begin your journey that way—but trust me, this strategy is not rewarding.

Good planning makes all the difference in how fast and far you will advance in your career. If you desire to seek out a new position or make a lateral career move, a well thought out, deliberate plan is a necessity. Some questions to consider when making your plan include:

- What kind of promotion are you looking for?
- Where are you willing to work or move?
- Are you willing to engage in a long commute?
- Do you know the job duties for various positions in administration?
- Have you taken the time to gain current letters of reference?
- Is your boss aware of your aspirations to move on?

Without a plan in place, your dream to gain a new job can end up in disaster. Let's work to address some of the steps required to create your game plan. Each step is discussed in depth and covers key focus areas.

DECIDE YOUR NEXT CAREER MOVE
Crossing Over

Working as an educational leader is one of the most rewarding careers in education. The potential to use your skills of teaching, sociability, creativity, and collaboration are endless. The potential to change the world for the better is priceless. Initial planning to move on to new career levels must include your awareness of four key areas I refer to as "Career Bridges." Bridges are the major pathways that most educators attempt to enter when moving to a new job in educational leadership. Each time I made a job move, I was aware of the prerequisites required to cross over to a new career level. I also knew that each area possessed unique challenges and hurdles. Let me further clarify theses four Career Bridges:

Career Bridges

Current Position Factors	New Career Level	Fear Factors
Teacher	Assistant Principal	Crossing over to the "Dark Side"
Assistant Principal	Principal	The buck stops with you
Principal	District Office Staff	We're here to help
District Office Staff	Superintendent	Can you walk on water?

31

Crossing over to the Dark Side:
Teacher to Assistant Principal

In most school districts, a principal is usually assisted by someone known as a vice-principal or assistant principal. Unlike the principal, this role does not have quite the decision-making authority as the principal. Although they still yield the same authority among students, assistant principals do not have the power of the principal.

Becoming an assistant principal is an exciting career move. The majority of assistant principals serve for several years, preparing for advancement to principal jobs; others are career assistant principals. An assistant principal is responsible for student discipline, attendance, scheduling student classes, ordering textbooks, supplies, and working with student achievement and support services. They also counsel students on personal, educational, or vocational matters.

In the majority of schools, assistant principals play a role working with teachers to provide interventions, developing new curricula, evaluating teachers, and coordinating school-community relations. The number of assistant principals that a school employs varies, depending on the number of students.

An assistant principal commented about her role as an administrator: "My job is demanding, fast-paced and filled with new challenges every day. I have so much to learn, which excites me. I'm on my feet most of the day talking with students and visiting classrooms, which I like because I'm not sitting at a desk all day. I don't know where the time goes. I love my job!"

As a teacher, becoming an assistant principal is the first step toward moving into administration. While a few teachers prefer to take baby steps before entering administration with jobs such as mentor teachers, department chairs, or activity directors, the majority of teachers enrolled in educational administrative programs prefer to leap directly to the role of assistant principal.

> **INSIDER TIP**
>
> Moving from teacher to administrator is a stimulating and rewarding growth experience. Find a mentor to guide you along the way.

The rank in file, however—your teacher friends—often have trouble with "one of their own" leaving the classroom to become an administrator. They often refer to your aspirations as, "Crossing over to the Dark Side... where those school administrators work." They provide daily reminders to those who flirt with the prospect of crossing over: "Why do you want to move over to the Dark Side? So you want to evaluate us and tell us what to do? Why would you want to leave us?" they ask, trying to keep you in the fold.

Crossing over from teacher to administrator presents the most challenges and is one of the toughest bridges to cross. As a teacher, it is critical to attend district and school wide committees to gain exposure to leadership.

For example, inform your site administrator(s) about your goal to become a school administrator. Tell them you are eager to learn leadership skills and need their help. Volunteer to complete the duty schedule, serve as a department chair, or lead a grade level or department meeting. Offer up your services, in order to gain access to opportunities that will help you learn more about leadership. Many graduate programs have fieldwork assignments that provide leadership experiences.

My former principal, now a superintendent and good colleague, recalls my eagerness to become an administrator. She often reminds me how willing I was to do whatever it took to get my hands on tasks that sounded like administration. I would offer to watch students after school, monitor passing periods, and develop programs to increase school attendance.

As a teacher, I knew I needed to learn more about the actual role of an assistant principal, so I requested personal days to "shadow" some assistant principals in our district. I used three personal days that resulted in quality "on the job" learning. On the third day, the assistant principal went home sick at lunchtime, and the principal asked me to fill in for the remainder of the day.

> **INSIDER TIP**
>
> Request a personal day to job shadow an assistant principal for the day to learn more about the job.

Now I had "acting assistant principal" experience and loved every minute of it!

In my experience, the most difficult part of crossing over from teacher to assistant principal is the fear of the unknown. Most teachers don't get access to leadership roles, working in a classroom. Trying to gain leadership experience as a teacher in a classroom, surrounded by thirty-five or more students, coupled with taking graduate classes at night can be a daunting task. I highly recommend finding a mentor, preferably an administrator at your site, who can encourage you to take on a new challenge and guide you along the way.

Fear, fatigue, and apathy can set in early, and I have found that teachers often give up the will to live during their quest to become an administrator. I have known enthusiastic teachers with the potential to become outstanding school administrators concede, "I just don't know... I don't think I want to leave the students!"

Juggling different roles and responsibilities, while trying to cross over from teaching to administration, calls for some expert planning. If you are a good teacher, you are undoubtedly a good planner. Use your skills to your best advantage during this critical period of transition. Make sure you don't neglect your students, by ensuring that you have monthly instructional plans developed and daily substitute plans ready, should you be called on to fill in for an administrator. Plan your days, weeks, and months out in advance, so you can be ready for the unexpected.

Another area that deters some teachers from entering administration is the length of the work day. Most teachers believe administration is a life threatening position. "How can I work all those hours?" they ask. Here's the real story—and I share this opinion openly.

As a teacher, I ended my day by planning for the next day's lessons, clearing off my desk, cleaning up the classroom, and stopping by the main office to pick up messages. Before going home, I would sit in my car for a few minutes before starting the engine. I needed to catch my breath. I was exhausted. Teaching six different lessons of math and science to students who needed me to be "on" every second took an incredible amount of energy. While I knew I wanted to be an administrator, I started to doubt myself. "How could I work any longer? These administrators have killer hours."

As an administrator, I did work longer hours—there was no doubt about that. But the hours were unlike a teacher's workday that was concentrated with no time to breathe. Administrator hours are spread out over the day. By that, I mean I could use the restroom whenever I wanted (big perk); could catch a cup of coffee or make a telephone call. It didn't take me long to learn that my job overseeing hundreds of students during and after school as an assistant principal was unlike that of a teacher, who was always accountable to a set group of students and confined in a classroom.

As an assistant principal, I would walk through classrooms every day, supervise lunch and monitor the passing of classes—all good exercise, in my opinion. At the end of the day, I was tired, but not the "drop dead" fatigue I experienced as a teacher. This is not a fact often shared by administrators, but it is the truth. Working as a school administrator is stressful and has long hours, but the job is not as exhausting as teaching in a classroom, constantly having to "be on" for every student. The job of an administrator is exciting and has a sense of freedom that enables one to withstand the stress of the job. Fortunately, when I became an administrator, I never forgot how tired I was as a teacher and always remembered that fact when asking a teacher to take on an "extra" duty.

Finally, teachers are often reluctant to move into administration, because they feel they will lose their connection with students. The loss of connections with students never happens in administration, if one is truly leading. I like to think, as an administrator, we teach all day, but our classroom is just larger, filled with students and teachers who need us.

In summary, crossing over from teaching to school administration certainly has its challenges. But a thoughtful plan that includes gaining leadership exposure, finding a mentor, and making the firm decision to become an administrator can provide a safe passage to one of the most rewarding jobs in education—that of leadership.

The Buck Stops with You:
Assistant Principal to Principal

There has never been a more opportune time to pursue a career as a school principal than now! There will soon be a principal shortage across the nation in our public schools, since most current principals are expected to retire within the next five years. The median income of a school principal is well above the national average, which can be an appealing aspect of the job. Although a principal must contend with many challenges and responsibilities, he or she is well compensated for the work. A high school principal typically makes more money than a middle school principal, while a middle school principal typically earns more than an elementary school principal.

A school principal is an instructional leader, who provides leadership to everyone (staff, faculty, students) in the school, while overseeing the day-to-day operations. The role of a school principal is that of guiding students and serving as a disciplinarian, when needed. It is a complex job that offers numerous challenges, with each day different from the day before. It is one of the most rewarding and exciting jobs in the field of education.

The principal of a school must not only possess leadership qualities but must serve as a manager. The principal will be involved with the hiring and evaluation of faculty and ensuring teachers are held to high standards. With teachers, a principal helps to develop and manage a working up-to-date curriculum that meets local, state and national standards. A principal is also responsible for preparing budgets and regular school status reports.

Although a principal dictates school policies, a principal does not have ultimate authority in that regard. The principal must respond to the needs and demands of the school board, parents and students. To that end, the principal must regularly meet with parents and address their many questions and concerns.

Most administrators decide to become a principal after serving three or four years as an assistant principal. I wanted to do it in one year. Two defining moments led to my quick ascension through door number two. First, I was assigned as an assistant principal of a middle school, serving with a veteran principal. Our leadership styles were similar, and I knew I would learn much from him. About the second week on the job, he asked me what my long term plans were. I immediately shared that I was eager to learn all I could but wanted to become a principal. "How will I do that?" I asked.

He smiled and replied, "It's easy. Watch me closely, listen to what I say, and most important, act like a principal. Don't act like an assistant principal," he warned, "act like me, the principal. Make decisions, be strong, be in control, create new programs, don't doubt yourself, be a leader, act like you are the principal."

Although his suggestions sounded too easy to be true, they actually worked. I followed his advice and began to act like him. I made decisions, dressed like a principal and led staff meetings. I acted like I was the principal—I loved it. I can't say that every principal you work for will share their leadership like this man did. I was fortunate in this respect. I do believe that most any principal would appreciate a decisive leader to help lighten the administrative load at the school site.

> **INSIDER TIP**
>
> Moving from assistant principal to principal requires knowledge of leadership principles, budget, decision making, and team building. Use your "on the job" training to learn these skills.

So, take my principal's advice on your own behalf. Increase your presence in your current role by "acting like a principal," and hopefully this strategy will increase your chances for a promotion sooner.

My second defining moment was unique, but I trust many administrators reading this book can relate to this instance. My principal directed me to sort out the disaster preparedness materials in a shed outside the main office. He had been putting this task off and really needed the help. "Would you mind getting on this right away?" he asked.

Reluctantly, I headed out to the shed and started the task. Unfortunately, I had dressed up for an earlier meeting at the district office and had worn one of my best suits. As I crammed into the shed, hauling water containers and cardboard toilets across the floor, I uncovered a squadron of spiders that decided to launch an attack on my legs. I managed to escape from the shed unharmed. Soaked in sweat, covered in dust, disgusted at the thought of spider bites and only four months into the job, I had a major career epiphany. I wanted to be a principal—and I wanted it *now!*

I believe there are two positions of leadership that have a high degree of control in our field: principals and superintendents. At that moment, dusting spider cobwebs off my legs, I knew I wanted to have more control over my career and how I spent my time as an administrator. I was ready to lead a school. And, I was ready to do what it took to get there. As a result of these two significant exchanges, I became highly motivated and determined to become a principal by the end of the school year. Think… do you have any defining moments of your own?

The next day I shared my "one year" plan with my principal, who quite frankly said, "Anything's possible, but no one in this district has ever accomplished that feat. With only one year of experience as an AP, I doubt you can move so quickly to a principal-ship."

> **INSIDER TIP**
>
> Assistant principals wanting to become principals must have experience in school budget and teacher evaluation. Ask your supervisor to give you experience in these areas.

Noting my disappointment, he added, "But on the other hand, you have shown me that you are ready to be a principal. You are very talented. I'd give it a try, if I were you," he said. "No harm, no foul. You could run a school."

I was elated. As a result of his encouragement, I did everything humanly possible to get promoted to a principal position. With only a few months left in the school year, I knew I had to step up my game plan. I volunteered for every committee that met after school and at the district office. I wanted them to notice me.

I joined our professional administrative organization and requested to be on a major task force. As part of my game plan, I decided to apply to outside districts, a move that could have boomeranged but fortunately did not. I alerted my principal to the fact I was applying to a few districts "closer to home." I thought he might share this information with those who mattered at the district office, which could potentially help me get promoted in my own district. My principal let me know that the district office was aware of my hard work. I liked working in Torrance and hoped they would not want to lose me to another district.

My plan to get a promotion in one year was successful, and I became the principal of a middle school in Torrance, providing eight years of school leadership. My desire to become a principal, with only one year of administrative experience, was a lofty goal. The first year was a challenge but a very rewarding learning experience.

Most assistant principals take more time to learn the ropes, since they know the school principal has direct responsibility for leading a school, and all matters fall on their shoulders. While serving as an assistant principal, they discover an all-encompassing theme; that "assistant" means "assist the principal." School principals, on the other hand, have the sole responsibility for what happens at their school. They have the sleepless nights and worries about maximizing long term goals for the school. They are in charge—and the "buck stops with them."

My former principal was very adept at taking ownership for his school. No matter how bad an incident got, he took responsibility. If a teacher had a bad day with a student, he provided more help. If students misbehaved at lunch, he sharpened up school monitoring protocols. My principal was an extremely collaborative leader and was responsible for everything that went on at his school. I want to emphasize that it only takes one interview to become a principal, but many days and nights to learn how to be a *great* principal.

Take caution, and be sure you are ready to move from your role as assistant principal to principal, and be certain you have the skills and the desire to take on the challenge. Learn everything possible as an assistant principal, and take on leadership roles at the site. Engage in as many district committees or task forces as you can, and increase your networking efforts.

> **INSIDER TIP**
>
> Ask a critical friend who knows your work history if they think you are ready to become a school principal.

More importantly, ask people you trust—a principal, director, or assistant superintendent—this key question, before taking the leap: "Do you think I'm ready to be a principal?" Hopefully, they will be candid and honest and share their thoughts about your talents and skills. They may encourage you to apply for in-house positions, or suggest you apply to other districts, or both. They may even suggest you wait another year or two. Whatever information you glean from those who know and care about you will be valuable.

We're Here to Help:
Principal to District Office

School districts face an endless barrage of problems. Among them is finding and retaining strong, responsible and enlightened leadership at the top. Mandated accountability measures, school security issues, outdated technology and school buildings, and the recent downgrading of social and economic conditions impacting students continue to affect the stability of our nation's schools. Fortunately, there is a growing consensus from school boards and the public at large that school districts need to hire the best, the brightest and most qualified leaders to lead our schools. Administrators working at the district level, however, are often not given clear roles and responsibilities. In addition, these top level leaders often lack the preparation to deal with the issues facing our schools.

A typical district office will employ coordinators, facilitators, administrators, directors, and assistant and deputy superintendents, as top level support staff. Some of these roles are clearly defined by the Board of Education and the superintendent.

> **INSIDER TIP**
>
> Quality administration is needed at the school district level. If your school has made significant growth under your leadership, consider work at the senior level to promote long term student achievement goals.

Most school districts will focus on two areas related to the job duties of district office administrative staff: (1) actions focused on improving student learning, and (2) organizing a school district in such a way to make that focus happen. So while the titles vary, know that if you are aspiring to becoming a district level administrator, you will be involved with the goal of supporting student learning.

Moving from a principal position to the district office is not for the faint of heart. These are coveted jobs. Once promoted to directors or assistant superintendents, these folks don't relinquish their appointments until retirement, demotion, or in some cases, advancement to the superintendency.

In my experience, there are two types of administrators who opt for district level positions: (1) those who decide to become superintendents and use a district level job as a direct career route, or (2) those who aspire to move beyond site leadership to become the best they can be in their particular area of interest.

Of course, we all know there are people promoted to district level positions, because they are tired of working at the site or those promoted by a superintendent, because they have "paid their dues."

These folks are in the minority but are probably most responsible for giving district offices mixed reviews, regarding its reputation.

After nine years serving as a principal, I began searching for a new challenge. In that time, I had earned my doctorate and was seriously thinking about becoming a school superintendent. I knew I needed to gain district level experience to actualize my career goals. While my colleagues kidded me that I had earned a "gig" at the DO, I refused to believe securing a position at the district office would be easy. Getting the job would be a huge challenge, since there were so few openings.

Why is it that school principals seem hesitant to move to the district office? In my opinion, I think it's because of the ambiguity about what goes on at the district office. I wondered myself, "What do these people do all day?" There are no students; there are a lot of cars in the parking lot, and from where I stood as a principal, tons of paperwork generated from those buildings. These thoughts plagued me for years and were an obstacle to overcome, before deciding to apply to district level work.

Schools are fun places to work, and as a principal, there's a lot of freedom to be gained from being in charge. I recall visits to the Torrance District Office. It was too quiet. Everyone seemed to whisper. From my perspective, the district office lacked spark and energy. It was very different from working at a school. It was a difficult question I had to answer. "Was this job one I actually wanted?"

Shortly after receiving my doctorate in organizational leadership, I decided it was time to seriously think about applying for assistant superintendent positions. I wanted to become a superintendent, and knew I would need district level experience to make that goal a reality.

Districts usually have three types of assistant superintendents on board: (1) human resources; (2) administrative services (finance, business, technology, facilities, food services); and (3) educational services (curriculum, instruction and student support services). Since the majority of my experience was involved with improving student achievement, a natural choice for me was to transition to a job related to educational services.

I scheduled a meeting with the district superintendent in January and informed him that I would be applying for assistant superintendent positions. He was not surprised, when I shared this news and appreciated my informing him in advance. He reiterated that he wished I could remain in his district as a leader and said he fully understood my desire to seek advancement. His three assistant superintendents were newly appointed, which, for me, translated to a lack of future openings.

As a result, I began applying for jobs within a 40 mile radius from home (my former 360 plan). Although my health was excellent, I was very aware that age is a factor and could impede my advancement to the superintendency. I decided I would take the risk and only apply to assistant superintendent positions, skipping over entry level coordinator, supervisor or director jobs housed at the district office.

Crossing over from principal to assistant superintendent was very difficult. First and foremost, there were very few job openings available at the time. Also, my resume needed updating and my school accomplishments, while commendable, had little connection to the work required at the district level. I knew that, until my resume linked site leadership experience with skills expected at the assistant superintendent level, gaining interviews would be a challenge. As an example, an accomplishment listed on my first resume sent to districts for assistant superintendent positions read:

- Created a student attendance program that increased student attendance from 95% to 96.5% in two years.

Rewriting this same accomplishment to resonate with district level experience helped me gain assistant superintendent interviews:

- Developed and executed a student attendance program, increasing student attendance from 95% to 96.5% in two years. Assisted district principals with implementing similar attendance programs at their schools.

As a result of my new resume, I was called and asked to interview for three jobs within a period of one week. The first interview was a nightmare. The drive to the district took well over an hour (located on the fringe of my 360 degree circle), and when I arrived in time for my appointment, I was asked to sit in a room with five other applicants.

I sat there for what seemed like an eternity and was then called to sit in another room to view a video. I was instructed to observe a teaching lesson and directed to draft (by hand) a brief teacher evaluation and plan for improvement, on the spot, within thirty minutes. I was then escorted to another room and instructed to prepare a short presentation to be delivered to the panel on school improvement techniques.

Finally, the interview time arrived, and I was informed that applicants would meet with two different panels. The entire process lasted well over three hours. I was later called back to interview with two other finalists, only to lose out to an "in-house" candidate, who I later learned had been awarded "Principal of the Year" in their district.

The next two interviews were a bit less complicated and again, I successfully made it to the finals, but lost out to in-house candidates. A month later, I realized the window of opportunity for applying to district level jobs was closing. I was happy at my school as a principal and resigned myself to wait until the following year and begin the process all over, since I was not willing to relocate.

My former boss, who had become a superintendent in another district, called excitedly to inform me she had an opening for an assistant superintendent of educational services. "Are you interested in applying?" she asked." Absolutely, I thought, and once again began practicing for an interview. About a week later, she called back, and the conversation went something like this:

Hello Marilou, I see from the applications I'm reviewing right now that you've put in an application for my assistant superintendent position. That's great, and I'm excited that you're interested in working with me again.

There are a few things I'd like to mention that I think are important. First, my director of categorical programs is retiring, and I'll be interviewing for that position, also. I've noticed in the stack of applications for the assistant superintendent job that I have some other very qualified people, who have also applied for this job.

You know Bob Smith—he's a director now, and he applied. Susan Jones has been a director of elementary education for the past six years and has applied. You know her too, right?

Well, here's what I think. While I still want to have you interview for the assistant superintendent position, why don't I make a copy of your application for the director opening, just in case. Are you all right with that?

Disappointed, but still composed, I thought for a moment and said, in a very professional manner, "I really appreciate your 'head's up' on this new information, but at this time, I am only interested in working as an assistant superintendent. So, while I thank you for your consideration, I will only apply for the assistant position."

This superintendent—a model of professionalism—said, "That's good to know, Marilou. Then I'll look forward to seeing you at the interview next week. My secretary will call you to arrange the interview specifics."

I had developed a plan for this phase of my career and believed it was important to stay true to the plan of moving directly from principal to assistant superintendent. The interview went very well, and I was appointed to be her assistant superintendent of educational services. *I was thrilled!* While not happy to leave a wonderful school district and great school, I knew that my move to assistant superintendent would be an exciting challenge and a job worth holding out for.

Having worked in many school districts, I knew the majority of site administrators were not avid fans of district office support staff. District office people tend to bring new ideas and programs to schools, which have a way of causing more work and stress for those working in the classroom. When teachers push back, district staff can be heard saying, "We're just here to help, so let us know what we can do to support you."

The "we're here to help" slogan is widely used in districts, and most site people are familiar with the phrase. As a newly appointed assistant superintendent of educational services, I was cautious to avoid using this slogan, with its negative connotations. I found this task difficult and caught myself several times in mid-sentence—*"I'm just here to…."*

To counteract this negative perception, I visited sites daily, asked questions, and worked with teachers to get them the tools they needed to be successful. I worked hard to gain their trust and respect, rather than force "my" programs into their classrooms. We worked together as a team to realize district goals.

> **INSIDER TIP**
>
> District office administrators have the potential to affect long term systemic change for a school district.

The negative attitudes generated toward positions and responsibilities at the district office often amaze me. We need exceptional educators to take on these pivotal roles, but because of the negative stigma, *good* people, who *should* work at the district office, don't apply.

I remember being very sensitive about the stigma, after becoming a district office administrator, myself. As an assistant superintendent, I hired two high performing teachers on special assignment. I managed to find them office space in a storeroom off the main corridor, near the restrooms. Eager about their new positions, they asked for permission to spend the weekend at the district office to decorate their space.

Arriving on Monday morning, I was excited to see what they had accomplished. As I walked into their new office, I was shocked! In one corner sat an artificial tree and several plants. Frilly curtains were hanging from the windows, and classical music was playing on a small stereo. A coffee station and snacks were displayed on a small table, and each teacher had a scented, lighted candle on their desk.

It was almost four o'clock in the afternoon, and I was aware that our teachers and administrators would soon arrive at the district office. I didn't want to disappoint these two women, but in the interest of time, I explained, "I know you're both excited about working at the district office—but what were you thinking? We can't have our teachers think there's a party going on in here. I know you want the office to look nice, but turn off the music, and blow out the candles. It looks like you're ready for the world's longest break, and I don't want our school people to think for a minute we don't work hard down here."

There it was, short and sweet. One of these women later became a principal, and whenever I meet with her, we joke about that day. She reminds me about my strong advice and the impact it has had on her, professionally.

Transitioning from principal to assistant superintendent was not easy. As a principal, I liked being in charge and enjoyed working at a school. I knew that getting acclimated to an "assistant position" again, to support the goals of the superintendent, might take some time. The transition was much easier than I thought it would be. While I really missed the students and teachers, I was able to leverage my time to visit schools and work with principals and teachers on programs that impacted students. I started to feel like I was a leader again, accomplishing good things for students. I finally knew I had made the right choice to a district office role, when I saw my efforts turn into increased student achievement on a district wide scale.

The prospect of leaving the site, with all its excitement and energy, can stand in the way of some very talented principals, who should move up to the district office. If you happen to be on the fence about applying for a district level position, keep in mind that the job is only as boring or devoid of students as you make it. Working at the district level affords one the opportunity to make a greater impact on students. If you decide to move to a district position, remember, you have two choices. Continue the "We're here to help" tradition, or work to make a difference for students, schools, and the community. The choice will be yours.

Can You Walk on Water?
District Office to Superintendent

To many—even educators in the field—the role of the school superintendent has always been a little mysterious. Most people know that the superintendent is the ultimate "person in charge," but what superintendents actually do remains vague. The majority of superintendents report that the superintendency for them was a calling, rather than a job. They believe they have an opportunity to impact and shape the lives of children, that can change the future in profound ways. They

> **INSIDER TIP**
>
> A superintendent's job is a lot like being a school principal. The only difference really is the size of the school yard. If you liked being a principal, you'll love the role of a school superintendent.

46

know the job is difficult and are keenly aware of how vulnerable they are in the the job (average tenure 2.5 years) but believe their "calling" and impact they have on society is compensation enough for all the hard work, stress and frustration they experience achieving their goals.[1]

What does a superintendent really do all day? In truth, as a new superintendent, I sometimes wondered. It soon became clear to me that society had placed much on my plate, and my power to influence stakeholders was very different from that of a principal.

State and federal mandates and special-interest groups placed a considerable burden on every decision I made, and the time spent with parents and teachers demanding a seat at the decision-making table made me think I had little or no power to effect change.

> **INSIDER TIP**
>
> Key skills to learn before becoming a superintendent include budget development, improving student achievement, communicating effectively, and building positive relationships.

Working with board members could take up the majority of a work day. These public officials often have contact with a wide range of stakeholders, who request "face time" on issues such as school construction, bell schedules, school bonds, boundaries, inclement weather, and curriculum and instruction. More importantly, the standards-based accountability reform movement was built into my evaluation, as a minimum expectation for the job.

It was a tough and complicated job, but I loved every minute of being a school superintendent. It was thrilling to be able to impact students in such a positive way. I spent each day knowing my actions would make a profound difference on the lives of students—and for me, that was all it took for complete job satisfaction!

Now for the fun part! The last time I reviewed a brochure for a superintendent position, it sounded something like this:

- Must know budget, finance, curriculum, special services, instruction, negotiations, personnel, evaluation, board

[1]Sashway, Larry. The Superintendent in an Age of Accountability. September. 2002. Eric Digest 161. <https://scholarsbank.uoregon.edu/jspui/bitstream/1794/3387/1/digest161.pdf>

- governance, facilities, transportation, food services, and career education.
- Must demonstrate excellent communication skills, budget development, strategic planning, community relations, success in improving instruction and student achievement, and working with special education mandates.
- Must show experience in grant funding, establishing and working with foundations, developing curriculum, working with outside funding sources, and creating community initiatives.
- Must have integrity, be trustworthy, be transparent, have a sense of humor, be able to work long hours, have stamina, understand and embrace technology, and be willing to live in and love our community.
- Must like kids.

Walk on water? Perhaps God is the only truly qualified candidate for the job!

All kidding aside, these job qualifications are real. If you have plans to move on to the top spot of leadership in a school district, congratulations are in order. In my humble opinion, it's the most rewarding job in the field of education.

Now about walking on water.... At the very minimum, you should be able to have an intelligent conversation about each of the job requirements listed above. For example, you don't need to be a budget expert, but you do need to be able to navigate and understand a district finance plan.

The soft skills, such as integrity, sense of humor, and being trustworthy are all part of the role. It is important to note that, if one is aspiring to the superintendency, spending time in a variety of seats throughout your career and working in different districts lends to building experience in these areas. It is also critical to be current with professional development in the areas of student learning, school law, and finance.

As the complexity of the job has increased, so have fears of a dwindling pool of qualified leaders. Research suggests there is an impending crisis on the superintendency. Many quality educators are shying away from moving on, and our nation's school districts are in desperate need of quality superintendents. As we know, students of varying backgrounds, ethnicity, and social economic status now fill our schools.

Clearly, districts are aware they need to respond to the special needs of a diverse and multi-ethnic population. But here's the news… by and large, the demographics of district leadership are still not reflected in most school districts. The top-level positions are overwhelmingly held by white males, in the latter half of their careers, and only about 14 percent of superintendents are women (this figure hasn't changed in 100 years). Only 5 to 10 percent of superintendents are nonwhite.

The reason for sharing this information is to point out that change is in the air. Impending student diversity in our schools has intensified an obvious and very public need to hire minority superintendents— superintendents who reflect the student demographics attending our nation's schools. Don't lose hope, if you are a woman or minority candidate, because there is an emergent window of opportunity for those desiring to move to this leadership top spot.

I worked for four years as an assistant superintendent and decided it was time to get serious about my ultimate goal of becoming a superintendent. I asked my boss, the superintendent, if she thought I was ready for the job. "Yes," she replied, "What's taken you so long?"

I updated my resume, attended our state's Superintendent Academy and continued to read current articles on the role of the superintendency, to better prepare myself for interviews. The first position I applied for was the superintendency in my own district, when my boss decided to retire. The district hired a prominent search firm to conduct the search and narrowed their final candidates down to four, one of them being myself.

I was extremely unaware of the workings of executive search firms at the time and was amazed that a district would pay over $40,000 for an outside firm to assist with the hiring process. I did not know that in-house candidates are rarely selected, when a board has hired a search firm. Boards that want one of their current assistant superintendents to assume the role of superintendent tend to appoint the next superintendent. I was devastated that the board chose another candidate. I was later informed by the consultant that I was a good candidate, interviewed well but lacked finance experience deemed important by the board.

As a result of this defeat, I became aware that I needed to gain more school finance experience, so I enrolled in a School Business Manager's Academy. I also decided to escalate my job search. At the time, I was place bound and could only apply to districts within my 360 degree commute window (40 mile radius). I applied to three districts, all of which gave me interviews, based on my paperwork.

The first two interviews were conducted by high profile search firms, and in each case, the job was awarded to a sitting superintendent. While I was informed I did very well on each interview, the consultants indicated the talent pool was currently filled with experienced superintendents, eager to work in or near Orange County, California, commonly known as the "Gold Coast."

On my third attempt, I interviewed and was called back by the consultant, informing me I had placed in the top two. After the final interview, the search consultant informed me that I had aced the interview and would be hearing from him soon. He winked at me as I left the district office and said, "I think this one's yours." I was happy with the news, but over the years, I have learned to keep excitement at bay.

That evening, the consultant called me, confirming once again that the board was ready to make a decision. He asked me what my salary parameters were for the job. I responded by saying, "Well the range is what's listed on the brochure $110,000-125,000, right?" He agreed, in which case I informed him I wanted to be "considered" for the higher range, if possible, since I was earning $118,000 at the time, as an assistant superintendent.

The next morning, he called to inform me the board had chosen the other candidate, as she was willing to take the job for $110,000. I was unnerved that he hadn't called me back, before deciding to inquire about my willingness to negotiate salary. I always wondered about his (and my) lack of honest and open communication during that search.

The next year, my husband and I decided we would take a risk and extend the job search to include other cities, which meant relocating.

We knew this decision would increase my chances of becoming a school superintendent. It was obvious to both of us that, if I were to realize my goal of becoming a superintendent during this lifetime, I would have to extend my 40 mile radius to cover the entire state.

It was a momentous decision on his part, but he knew how much I had worked toward gaining this leadership role. As a result, I applied for a large unified district in Fresno County and was selected to serve as their first woman superintendent. I was thrilled and worked for four wonderful years, before making another move to a high school district closer to our home in Orange County.

Crossing over into the superintendent position is a complex process. The district usually works with a consulting firm, hired by the Board of Trustees to coordinate and oversee an executive search. Once again, it is also important to have a critical conversation with a trusted friend or colleague, who knows your work, talents, abilities and track record. Ask them if they believe you have what it takes to be successful in the role as superintendent.

After determining if you want to begin this journey, find a mentor —perhaps a retired superintendent—or hire a professional in the business of mentoring. I personally hired a consulting firm to work with me on interviewing and resume building for the superintendency and found the learning experience invaluable.

Preparing for the superintendency can be an avocation, all its own. It's a lot of hard work and time. Results do not come in overnight. A search can continue for six months. The average superintendent interviews six times before gaining their first position. It takes time to learn about the school district, determine if the job and district are a good fit, and then apply for the position. Most of the energy for gaining a superintendent position is focused to address the needs of the district and being able to express confidence in the interview. These issues will be discussed in detail in the chapter on Preparation - Practice Makes Perfect.

PLAN YOUR STRATEGY

With an awareness of the four Career Bridges (p. 31), it's now important in the planning process to decide what position you want to apply for. Use feedback from your critical friends to target jobs that match your skill set and experience. Find a range that works for you.

For example, if you are a teacher, you will probably target vice principal, assistant principal, teacher on special assignment, or teaching assistant principal positions. There are a variety of career ladders that will meet your requirements. Also, selecting a particular job can be dependent on timing issues. We'll talk about these below.

Location, Location, Location

Deciding where to apply can present a challenge. In the introduction, I wrote that I applied to districts for assistant principal within forty miles from my home. I was eager to transition from teacher to administrator and did not want to wait for a job to open up in my current district. It was a gamble I was willing to take—and fortunately, it paid off.

Some educators are "place bound." Others are willing to move to another state or city to gain an administrative position. These issues are personal and should be carefully considered before making applications. Consideration of family members, financial concerns, and long term life plans also play into the decision of relocation.

As you develop your plan, you must also consider the type of district you want to apply to. For example, if you are currently working in a high wealth district and have no experience working with inner-city youth, you may want to consider how this will play out in your interview and in your career, if you were to get the job.

Throughout my career, I applied for jobs in different types of school districts and secured positions in both high-wealth and deep inner-city school districts. I believe that remaining in one type of district has the potential to limit access to the full spectrum of jobs offered. Employers frequently want to hire applicants with a wide range of experience working with different populations and social-economic groups. They know that applicants who bring a varied background to the table are able to approach educational issues from many different perspectives.

These Wheels are Made for Driving

Long commutes are tough! It's one thing to say you'll apply for jobs within a forty mile commute—and another to get the job, and actually drive it. If you extend the boundaries of your search, be realistic and ask yourself, "Can I drive a lengthy commute every day?" The drive may look easy on paper, but another story altogether, when the road map turns into freeway.

I loved my job in Torrance Unified but endured a long commute, for a total of two hours each day. When it rained or an accident occurred on the freeway, my commute time could double. Relocating was not an option (son in high school, husband commuting the other direction). So I chose to endure a long commute, and honestly it was hard on my family, in addition to being physically exhausting. I put 100,000 miles on my Toyota and listened to books on tape every day.

I encourage you to weigh the pros and cons about commuting, before you apply for and accept a job far from home. Don't convince yourself that you'll "only take the job for one year." That approach to problem solving seldom works. Once settled into a new job, most people establish close ties to their district and abandon all thoughts of leaving. A one-year stint doesn't play well on a resume, either.

I've been asked many times, if I had the decision to make all over again, would I still accept a position in Torrance, knowing how tough the commute would be. My answer: "Absolutely!"

I've Got a Plan—and I'm Sticking to It!

Once you have your plan in place, regarding position, where to locate, and type of school district, it is important to remain true to your plan. Be aware that a limited plan (waiting for a position to open up in your own district) may significantly increase the timeframe to actualize your career goals. The more open the plan (willing to relocate and work in a variety of districts), the quicker one may become promoted.

Some candidates struggle with an internal age factor and believe they don't have time to wait three or four years for the perfect opportunity to open up. They have the desire and the skills to become an administrator and want to make the move as soon as possible.

I recently taught a graduate course to teachers aspiring to school administration. One man was approaching fifty-eight and was determined to become an assistant principal. I asked him his plans about transitioning from a teacher to administrator in a district he had worked for over 30 years. "I'm not naïve," he said. "I want this new leadership position real bad, and I know I need to apply anywhere in California, if this is going to happen for me."

If you have similar desires, open up your window of opportunity, by extending your search to include different job classifications, districts, and locations. It is important to develop momentum, to keep your plan moving forward.

To Tell or Tell—That is the Question!

Okay, now that you have a plan, the next thing to consider is developing your communication strategy. Here's the thing—let me explain. If you keep the plan to yourself, you risk creating problems for yourself at work!

Behinds Closed Doors

It is important to share your plan, as a way to let your immediate supervisor know of your desire to advance in your career. This is a risky and delicate issue that must be handled properly. It is important to never let your supervisors find out you are interviewing for a new position on their own. In my estimation, I believe that there is a 95% chance your employer *will* discover you are applying out—so why risk it?

Prospective new employers will call to enquire about your qualifications, or your colleagues at work will be eager to let them know. Your boss needs to be apprised of any changes in his staff, if he is to be considered a good manager, himself. He doesn't want to be blindsided and embarrassed with his board or out in the community.

Consider timing issues. How long have you worked at your current position? Is your boss in any transition, herself? Are you in good standing with your boss? Are you in the middle of a project that needs completing?

Sit down and make a list of all the variables that could put your boss in a bad place. Strategize how to deal with each issue. For example, if you are in the middle of any high visibility projects, assure your boss that you will work to complete the projects yourself, or spend time with your replacement to make sure they can complete them on time. If you haven't been on the job long, prepare to discuss why you want to move on so soon.

Make an appointment with your supervisor to share your plans about your career advancement goals. Additionally, if you are close to gaining a position, alert your boss about any job specifics. If you feel a job offer is forthcoming, prepare a statement in advance, with your boss, to inform the organization. Follow your boss' lead. After all, your supervisor will receive a call from the hiring district to inquire about your qualifications, job performance, and integrity and having an open dialog with your boss will more likely lead to a positive resolution for all parties concerned with your transition.

Ready or Not—Here I Come!

Announcing to everyone that you are looking for a promotion works well for highly talented individuals. This strategy also works well for teachers deciding to transition to administration and assistant principals and district office staff looking to advance. They make it well known they want to move up, and tell people candidly about their plans.

This tactic can also help neighboring districts become aware of your intentions and increase your potential for recruitment. This strategy, however, is not advisable for principals or superintendents. Staff, community, and district workers tend to rely heavily on these administrators, especially if they are successful. If stakeholders learn their leader wants to "leave them," a new set of problems will develop.

For example, if a principal broadcasts their intention to become an assistant superintendent, the news travels fast, and soon it becomes difficult to bring in assignments or convince staff to take on new projects. The same holds true for current superintendents desiring to move to other superintendent positions. When the organization discovers their superintendent is searching for another position, fear sets in.

When I decided to move to a new challenge, after serving four years in one school district, I discretely shared this information with the board president. She knew if the community became aware of my plans to leave, the stability of the district would be compromised, which had the potential to impact the district's chances to pass a general obligation bond.

Stability is priority number one for school districts, and a superintendent moving on to another district threatens that stability.

Word of Mouth

People who work in the field of education, especially school districts, are very well connected. The pipeline is fluid, and news travels fast. If you badmouth a current employer, that information travels fast and may hurt your chances for promotions. It's a small world, and it's important to maintain your professionalism and not put your career in jeopardy.

The same holds true for social networking. Hosting a blog, a personal website, or an account on a social networking site can impact your job search—for better or for worse.[2]

I recently read a blog in which the creator wrote he lies in interviews. That wouldn't thrill a prospective employer, if they knew about it. Another job seeker's blog mentions that she loves to party all night, drinks to excess on a regular basis, hates her boss, and steals office supplies on occasion. Again, this is not a profile that would excite most employers.

Be aware that prospective employers are taking time to read your Facebook accounts and are checking in on your personal websites or blogs. It's now common practice for employers to "Google" people they are interested in hiring.

If your personal website address is listed on your resume, make sure it deals with your professional career and not personal information. One hiring manager I spoke to always looks at an applicant's website, if it's listed. Another told me that she would try to find out as much about a candidate as possible, including searching the person online.

Here are some Facebook, Website, and Blog Do's and Don'ts:

- Don't include a link on your resume to any site that includes content that is not appropriate for a business audience.

- Be very careful what you put online. If you have a MySpace or Facebook account, people you won't want to be reading your profile may be able to access it, even if you think nobody will read it. Make your account private, so only your friends can access it. Be extra careful, and don't post anything that you don't want a prospective employer to read.

[2]To Blog or Not to Blog? How Blogging and Social Networking Can Impact Your Job Search by Alison Doyle, About.com Guide

- Be mindful of what you write. Just about anything that is online can be read by someone—or everyone. If you don't want the world to read what you've posted, make sure they can't.

- Blogging and using Facebook can become a passion, but don't let that passion hinder your employment prospects. Keep blogging and communicating through Facebook—but blog safely, securely and carefully, so your career opportunities aren't jeopardized.

Seal of Approval:
References and Recommendations

The terms "recommendation letter" and "reference letter" are often thought as one; however, there are real differences between the two terms.

- **Letters of recommendation** are very specific in nature and are always addressed to a specific individual. They are written for a specific job category, usually written by supervisors. Letters of recommendation are the letters requested in most job applications.

- **Letters of reference** are more general in nature and are usually addressed, "To Whom It May Concern." Throughout your career, it is important to ask individuals who have worked with you to write a letter of reference. For example, when I attended graduate school, I asked the dean to write me a letter, commenting on my performance and initiative. I also asked board members from various districts that I worked to write me general letters of reference for my portfolio.

Here are some tips to explain why these letters are important and corresponding tactics to navigate the process:

- Request letters from former supervisors, colleagues, board members, university professors, on a regular basis.

- Offer to send your reference people a brief list of your accomplishments and work history. Do this through email, or send them a copy of your resume.

- Some people that you request letters from like to suggest that you write the letter for them, offering to sign it when completed. Try not to resort to this tactic too often. Try to encourage your reference to complete some prearranged "boiler plate" comments, by leaving blank areas for them to fill in, for the sake of authenticity.

- Ensure that every letter is dated. Dateless letters frustrate paper screeners. They may speculate you are trying to cover up something. If you have a dateless but good recommendation letter, ask the author to update it.

- Keep your file current throughout your career, especially when working with new supervisors. It may be impossible to request a recommendation from someone who supervised you ten years ago. One of my best letters of reference came from my Torrance superintendent, when I was a principal. Two months after he wrote my glowing letter, he passed away.

- Ask for signed copies of all letters, so you can make a PDF file or make hard copies. Many districts request only PDF files, when using the online application process, and PDF files are a requirement.

- You will be asked to list 3-5 people as references on a job application. These people may not have written you letters of recommendation but should be willing to speak on your behalf, if contacted. For example, I asked the county superintendent if he would write me a letter of recommendation. He said, "Better to use my name as a reference on your application, since I know they will call me." This was good advice, since his report to those who later called him actually got me hired!

- Ensure your references speak positively about you. Don't list someone on your application who might compromise your chances of getting hired. If your current superintendent or boss won't speak highly of you, list a possible board member, community member, or assistant superintendent who will.

- Important—always let your references know they may be called.
- Don't send in a reference letter, just because you have it. Make sure your letter is exceptional and speaks very well about you and your abilities. If you have lackluster letters, it's best not to use them, unless you have nothing else. These letters are always read, since employers like to hear how well others think of you.
- Most applications request three to five current letters. I once received a packet from an applicant that contained over fifty letters of recommendation. A general rule of thumb is to send two to five over the number requested, but only if these letters are exceptional. If you only have two or three exceptional letters, only send the required amount. Don't send extras for the sake of sending, unless they address some specific areas of concern to an employer that may not have been covered in better letters.
- Application protocols always request letters of recommendation from those who have directly supervised you. If you don't comply with instructions included in the application packet and only send letters from colleagues, students or parents, your application will not be taken seriously. You need letters from those who have evaluated you and have observed how you have handled working under pressure.
- If you have exceptionally good letters from your supervisors, a letter from a good colleague, parent or student can add another positive dimension to your application. A superintendent friend recently shared that a deciding factor for his last hire was based on a heartfelt note written by a student for him when he was a teacher.
- If you receive a letter that is poorly written or rife with typos, do the person a favor and let them know. Most of us in education would be extremely embarrassed if we realized our letter was riddled with typos or grammatical errors. Many of us write these letters in a hurry, and typos can be an unfortunate result of this haste.

Parting Shots

Earlier in this book, I stated that many qualified candidates, who have the potential to move into key educational leadership roles, do not want to take on these assignments. Some of the reasons for their hesitancy to move into school leadership include ambiguity about the various job duties, lack of knowledge about the ascension process, and little or no information on how to navigate the employment interview.

This chapter was designed to add clarity to some of those concerns. Not only is this a book to help qualified people gain access to top positions of leadership, but this book also serves as a resource to encourage those on the fence, who may be considering these jobs.

School districts need intelligent, creative, and courageous leadership at the top, if our schools are to thrive and positively impact our children's futures.

Key Planning Actions

- Decide what jobs you want to apply for.
- Be cognizant of—but not totally affected by—negative rhetoric directed toward a particular job category.
- List specific knowledge, skills and abilities necessary for the job.
- Complete required certification, specialized training or education to enhance your professional skill set.
- Decide on a timeline to reach your immediate or long-term goals.
- Decide where you will apply and if you are willing to engage in a long commute.
- Create a communication plan to alert your supervisor of your intentions to seek new employment.
- Seek out and obtain references and recommendations.

After reading through this chapter, I'm hopeful you've learned more about the process of seeking out a new position and getting promoted. Once you've focused and have strategies in place to steer you in the right direction, it's time to prepare for the next steps in the application process.

In the next chapter, "Packaging - The Art of Self Promotion," I will point out specific tips to help you get to the interview table. Congratulations on your decision to take on a new challenge in your career!

Section III:
PACKAGING - The Art of Self Promotion

"Unless a man is able to 'sell' himself and his ideas, unless he has the power to convince others of the soundness of his convictions, he can never achieve his goal. Unless he can persuade others that his ideas are good, he will never get the chance to put them into effect."
~ Robert E.M. Cowie

Hopefully, as you've been reading, you have also been working on your plan to secure a new position of leadership. You're half way there and probably now visualizing the finish line. There are plenty of inspirational messages designed to help us during our journey. "You can't win, if you don't play the game" is one of mine that I referred to when contemplating career advancement. Another favorite of mine is, "You can't get promoted, if you don't get to the interview table."

Self-promotion—or what I call great packaging—is one of the most critical components of the promotion process. I can't stress this fact enough. You may have outstanding credentials, stellar recommendations, exceptional experience and killer confidence, but if your paperwork reads poorly, you can forget about the interview and the promotion!

Conversely, if your paperwork is well written and stands apart from the others, you will most likely be offered an opportunity to interview. Ninety-nine percent of the applicants called for interviews in educational leadership have outstanding paperwork.

As you fill out your application and create your letter of interest and resume, keep in mind that these important tools are the communication link between you and the school district, for the sole purpose of influencing, informing and persuading them to hire you. Your paperwork holds the most prominent place in the job search. It acts as your foot in the door, the first contact and therefore the single most important step to gaining an interview.

THE DEVIL'S IN THE DETAILS

Remember my chart referred to in the Introduction? As you begin your journey, you'll need to record everything you do. You must create a system to track the job particulars, and include specific information regarding each search. Here's a sample chart you can replicate on your own:

Job Tracking Form

School District and Address	Application Date and Documents	Position	Phone Email Website	Main Contact	Record of Phone Contacts	Interview Date	Estimated Salary and Benefits
California School District	06/01/11 District App. Cover Letter Resume	High School Principal	310-555-0999 bjones@ab.org www.CA.usd	Barb Jones Director HR	05/12/11	06/30/11	$110,000.00

Under each category list additional information:

- The full district address, telephone number, email and main contact
- Where you found the job posting
- Method of application (i.e. online or U.S. Mail, FedEx)
- Key contacts in district
- Projected time frame for interview
- Notes from the interview
- Specific salary information (does salary include health and welfare benefits, or is there an employee contribution?)

Another form I developed was a networking tracking form. Basically, this form catalogs influential contacts from your work life, such as mentors, community liaisons, business and professional contacts. This list of networking associates will be a great resource to you.

For example, once during a job search a district requested that I email them the names of five people not included on my application whom they could contact for references. They wanted the list in one hour. "Yes," I said, "one hour."

I simply took out my tracking form and selected people who would make me shine when called to speak on my behalf. Their names and contact information were at my fingertips, and the district requesting this information was impressed with my efficiency and timely response.

Save this form, and continue to update your list, even if you move on to another administrative position. These people will be valuable resources throughout your tenure in education and even into retirement.

Networking Tracking Form

Contact	Date Met and Event if Applicable	District or Company and Address	Email and Phone Number	Potential Reference	Notes to Help You Remember

In addition to developing job and contact tracking forms, I highly recommend that you begin to assemble a three-ring notebook to organize job specific information. I still use the same notebook I developed over twenty years ago. This notebook was extremely important in that it enabled me to study specific questions and review district information right before interviewing. The notebook also included updated resumes and letters of recommendation.

My notebook had everything in one place and served as my "career" Bible, when making applications, interviewing, and following up after interviews. I can't stress the importance of being organized, when looking for a new job—so begin to develop your notebook now!

Make a table of contents and include the following categories on your divider tabs:
1. Resume
2. Cover Letter Template
3. Professional Networking and Contacts
4. Current District Information (test scores, demographics, news articles of your accomplishments, important certificates, etc.)

5. Interview Questions (template and answers—more about this in chapter on Preparation)
6. Job Tracking Form

SHOW ME THE JOBS

The window of opportunity for job openings in educational leadership ranges from February through late summer. Of course, openings come up throughout the school year, but if you intend to begin a job at the start of the school year, the second part of the school year is considered the traditional application window.

Every state has online job boards, usually hosted by state or county offices of education. If you don't know the names of your state's job boards, search for them on the internet, by choosing key words, such as "educational administration, name of state, school district, assistant principal, job openings." You may be required to join the job board, by setting up an email and password account. Check these boards every few days, and sign up for job alerts, if they offer that feature.

Each state has its own method for communicating job openings, and you should check them regularly for updated postings. These jobs are never secret and should not be difficult to locate. When searching for superintendent openings, there are many state and national search consulting firms that regularly list district openings, which can be found with an internet search.

I encourage you to step away from your computer and venture out of your office, now and then. Try to get a jump on prospective administrative openings within your county, by networking to learn about possible future leads. You can also discover prospective openings through your involvement in professional organizations and county steering committees or task forces. Mentors will also alert you, when they hear about an opening that may be a good fit for you. In summary—make good use of the internet and network to find job postings as your primary search vehicle.

NOTHING PERSONAL:
The Paper Screening

The pre-screening process allows a school district to narrow down their pool of applicants to those who are the best fit for the position. Anyone can look good on paper, but a thorough pre-screening can separate the most appropriate applicants from all the others and enables employers to focus their interview process on only the most appropriate candidates.

School district pre-screening takes a variety of forms, from ad hoc committees convened by the superintendent or director of human resources to a solitary pre-screening event orchestrated by one person. Typically, if a committee is formed, members who work in the targeted job category are asked to serve, and they control who is granted an interview.

I have served on many pre-screening committees throughout my career. Below, I have bulleted some comments overheard from colleagues during pre-screening sessions that resulted in paperwork being placed in the "not so interested pile."

- I can't read the font—does this person think I'm twenty or what?
- This man applies for everything that moves. I've seen his name listed as an applicant for every position in this district.
- Where are the dates on these reference letters?
- What exactly has this person done? I can't tell from the resume.
- This person looked good on the resume but then wrote a poem for her letter of introduction.
- Five page resume—and the guy's a teacher.
- Weird email: lovetomessaround@yahoo.com
- No degrees listed.
- I'm getting a headache... this letter has four pages.
- A one page resume for a superintendent?
- Wow, this candidate has really skipped around... six districts in three years.
- Where's the cover letter?
- Where's the application form?

- This person wrote she attended Stanford on the application, but I can't find it anywhere on her resume.
- This applicant doesn't list any accomplishments.
- I can't find the date when this person left his last district or if he is still employed.
- Listen to what this guy wrote: "I am an unmarried male looking to make more money in education."
- I can't believe it. I just counted 36 "I's" in this resume.
- Didn't listing height, weight and hobbies go out of style in the '70s?
- Funny typo here: Worked in "pubic" relations.

Are you beginning to get the point? Paper screeners have a tough job and need to read through the paper work, to determine if the applicant's skill set matches the job requirements. They will be focused on finding errors and omissions.

INSIDER TIP

Read sentences backwards to find hidden typos.

Screeners also look for clarity, accomplishments, and examples that show quantitative success. Rather than listing that you have "good problem solving skills" a paper screener is more likely to respond positively to your resume, if you talk about specific problems solved while working in your current district.

LET THE GAMES BEGIN

Hopefully, your job tracking and networking forms are made (and filled out), and you now have the beginnings of a career notebook. You have a plan in place and have identified districts you want to work for and know the range of leadership positions within your skill set. Now comes the serious work.

Most school districts require three main components to apply for a position: (1) application form; (2) letter of interest or introduction; and (3) resume.

There are different ways that districts require applicants to submit their application materials. Some of these include:

1. Using an official job online service (often state sponsored)
2. Using their own job online service (district created)

3. Receiving through the district's email
4. U.S mail or in-person delivery

In the United States, the majority of job seekers look for positions in companies that use online services to facilitate the application process. Loss of revenue and fiscal cutbacks for school districts have resulted in substandard technology. As a result, many school districts don't use online job services and still prefer the old fashioned way of receiving paperwork—snail mail or in-person delivery.

For districts that use an official employment job board, be aware of the following guidelines. When applying online, copy and paste your plain-text resume into appropriate fields. The school district will never see your (original hard copy) resume, until you hand it over in your interview. In order to turn your resume into a plain text document, you must conform to the following:

Converting a Word Document to ASCII Text[3]

Spell check and then re-save your resume in your word processing program (e.g. Word) before you move to the next step.

1. Open a simple text editor like Notepad (on the PC, under Start > Programs > Accessories > Notepad) or SimpleText (on the Mac).

2. Start Word (or your word processing program, if you're not using Word), if it is not already open.

3. In Word (or your word processing program), open the file for your resume. If you make any changes, be sure to double-check your spelling and grammar, before you save the file.

4. Highlight* all the text in your Word document, by clicking on Edit > Select All; or by using your mouse to run from the top of the file to the bottom; or on your PC, hold down the Control and the "a" keys simultaneously.

*Highlight. You will know that the text is highlighted, because the background and letters of highlighted content are in reverse from their normal state (black background with white letters is the highlighted state for normal black letters on a white background).

[3]JobHunt. 20 January 2012. < http://www.job-hunt.org/resumeASCII.shtml>

Note: Don't let your mouse "touch down" anywhere in the document's window, or the highlighting will go away, and you will have to start over again.

5. Copy the highlighted text into your computer's temporary storage (the "clipboard" on a PC) by clicking on Edit > Copy; or on your PC, press the Control and the "c" keys simultaneously.

6. Move to your simple text editor, most probably Notepad (step 1 above), and paste the copy of your resume file into this new editor. Click inside the Notepad window, and then click on Edit > Paste; or on your PC, press the Control and the "v" keys simultaneously.

7. Save as plain text. Select File > Save As, and then name the file resume.txt (or whatever.txt).

8. You aren't done yet! You need to adjust the text to make it more readable and interesting. You will notice that your resume, in Notepad, is not as "pretty" as it was before. That's because it is now plain text. All special formats, like boldening and italicizing, have been removed, as have any graphics or other non-text elements. (Now you know why it is called "plain" text!) This is a good thing! At least, for e-mail, it is. You can, and should, take some steps to improve the way ASCII text looks. It still won't be beautiful, but it will be more acceptable.

School districts not affiliated with a job board or able to host their own online application process, often request that applicants submit their resumes and attachments electronically through simple email. Here are some suggestions to use when undertaking email submissions:

- Follow all deadlines. If a district states they want all materials received by Friday at 3:00 PM, don't assume your application will be accepted if you send it at 3:15. Districts take timelines seriously, and I have never known one to accept a late application.

- Double check the employer's requirements. Do they want a copy of your administrative certificate? Do they want transcripts? You must provide the employer with everything required, or risk being eliminated.

- Photo copied transcripts are fine for initial job applications. Remember that official transcripts take time to secure from universities. I suggest you order a few in advance, in case you need to deliver them to speed up the hiring process, if offered a position.

- Try to send your files in PDF format. That way, all your work will stay intact, and you don't have to worry about plain text or reformatting issues.

- Name your attachment files appropriately. For example, title your attachments with your last name (i.e. ryder_resume; ryder_letter_of_introduction; ryder_reference_letter_01). Be sure to include the extension .doc or .pdf, so the reader can open it easily.

- Call the office where you are sending your materials to confirm delivery. Some emails have spam filters that can block your materials. For example, many school districts do not accept emails from Yahoo accounts and have a blocking system in place. Be sure to call or ask in your email for confirmation of receipt. Do not wait past the application deadline to confirm receipt.

The Application Form

The majority of school districts require applicants to complete district made application forms. Here are some guidelines to navigate this process:

- Download the form from the district website if offered, and complete their application online. Some districts do not have the software that allows direct entry online, so download and save the form to your computer. Be mindful—some of these forms do not allow saving and must be sent directly to the district upon completion. This irregularity can cause frustration, so check immediately to see if the document is savable, before inputting your information. If it isn't, you need to be prepared to complete the form in one sitting, since you cannot save your work.

- If you must complete an application form on paper—yes, this happens—use black ink, and print neatly.
- Complete the application form in its entirety. Do not leave anything out or use the words "see resume."
- Try not to abbreviate, but it's acceptable if space is limited.
- Do not aggrandize accomplishments or degrees. Ensure the information on your application form matches that on your resume. Double check.

> **INSIDER TIP**
> Never lie or stretch the truth.
> NEVER-EVER.
> It's not worth it.

- No typos or misspellings. One typo could land your paper-work in the reject pile. Proof, proof, proof.
- The application must be neat, correct and consistent with your resume. It's a form, so treat it like one.

Letter of Introduction

Most school districts require candidates to submit a letter of introduction (sometimes called letter of intent or cover letter) stating why they are interested in the position, qualifications and intent to officially apply to the district. This letter is extremely important and is used in educational administration to determine an applicant's personality as well as their credentials.

More importantly, the letter of introduction is an opportunity to quickly introduce yourself and catch the employer's attention. Much like the resume, it's another opportunity to market your skills to the screening committee, encourage them to read your resume, and grant you a job interview. Employers use the letter to also gain an understanding of how you write, think, and organize your thoughts. So take time when composing this letter, and do some homework on the district or position, before writing the letter.

WINNING PLAYS FOR LETTERS OF INTRODUCTION

Tip #1: Explain what you are applying for:

I am writing to express my formal interest in the position of principal for the Union School District. (or)

Please accept this letter as my intent to apply for the position of principal for the Union School District.

Tip #2: Share some job history:

*My experiences in education have been wide and diverse. I have worked in three school districts and two states, **gaining a breadth of experience from my involvement with many multi-cultural and socio-economic groups**. My experiences have included classroom teaching and site administration, as well serving at the district level as assistant superintendent of educational services and currently as district superintendent.*

Tip #3: Tell the district why you want the position:

Your district provides the perfect opportunity for a new career challenge. I believe my strengths and skills are a perfect match for those required for the principal of California High School.

Tip #4: Summarize some recent accomplishments:

Student Achievement: *Significantly improved student achievement in three school districts, through the implementation of professional learning communities, data driven instruction, and best practices in education.*

Tip #5: Use data to show success for accomplishments:

Student Engagement: *Implemented a district wide student attendance program—EveryDay Counts—increasing student attendance from 95.1% to 97 %. District revenue increased approximately $1 million, while students gained over 83,500 additional hours of classroom instruction in one year.*

Tip #6: Share your strengths:

Throughout my career, I have demonstrated integrity and honesty, in addition to maintaining a sense of humor, often required for today's school leaders.

Tip #7: Add some heartfelt information:

I believe passionately in public education. As an advocate for children and students, I believe that everyone involved with schools— everyone—must work together to ensure excellence in teaching and learning. Our children deserve no less.

Tip #8: Conclude with a polite goodbye. This is just another way to stand out and show your personality.

Thank you for taking the time to read my letter. I would honor the opportunity to meet with you during a personal interview to share more about my background, experience and vision for our schools. I am ready to excel in your organization. Thank you for reviewing my candidacy.

One word of caution... School districts are still very conservative organizations. Many resume books and websites recommend that you use creative fonts, drawings, or startling opening statements, to gain the reader's attention. I suggest you resist using flagrant, creative tactics from your professional written repertoire, unless you have sophisticated graphic design skills or are a skilled copywriter.

> **INSIDER TIP**
> The format of your cover letter such as typeface and graphics should match your resume.

Note: Most districts want creative thinkers on their team, but they also want school administrators, who can be role models for our youth, and be perceived in the community as traditional, public servants. If you cross that subtle line—you may be considered a rogue.

Attempt to keep your letter conversational, and let the reader know who you are more, as a person. In today's ultra-competitive job market, it is important to have an effective cover letter. First impressions are important. Make yours count!

BRAGGING RITES:
The Resume

In today's world, we all need a powerful resume. The game is played inside. You must get through the door. I can't stress this fact enough with educators: The resume is a tool with one specific purpose —to gain entry to the interview. A resume is an advertisement; nothing more, nothing less.

An effective resume should read a lot like a great advertisement. Typically, an advertisement is created to convince you that, if you buy a particular product, you will get these specific, direct benefits. Your resume must present you in the best light and should convince the employer you have what it takes to be successful and how the district will benefit from what you have to offer.

Write your resume to create *interest*, to persuade the employer to call you. If you write with that goal in mind, your final product will be very different than if you write just to inform or catalog your job history.

As mentioned earlier in this book, you should be continually updating your resume, as a *work in progress*. Save the resume template on your desktop, so you can regularly update recent accomplishments and achievements. There are thousands of books on the market that help people write resumes, and reading them can be overwhelming, since they give conflicting advice. In addition, services exist online to actually write a person's resume.

Don't succumb to the temptation of paying someone to write your resume!

As an executive mentoring consultant, I have worked with hundreds of educators to help them perfect their resumes. Some plead, "Please—just write it.... I'll pay you anything."

I refuse to write a person's resume, because I strongly believe they need to write it in their own words. When people create their own resume, they put their professional stamp on it, and create a unique document that sets them apart from others.

In an interview, when asked to respond to certain questions, an applicant who has created their own resume will be able to respond effortlessly about accomplishments and experiences, because they have been internalized in fine detail. They have proof-read, spell-checked, and wordsmithed every sentence.

When the going gets tough in an interview, applicants who have authored their own resumes will be able to deftly recall and state their experiences for use as examples throughout the interview. It's as simple as that. The resume, while a powerful door opener, can also serve to lay the groundwork for success in an interview.

I recall one of my clients sending me his resume for review. He complained, "I'm not getting any interviews, and I paid two hundred dollars for an online service to write this for me. Why I am being overlooked?"

I reviewed his top dollar document and couldn't believe what I was reading. His resume read as if he were applying for a position at the United Nations, rather than assistant superintendent. The resume writing service elevated his modest achievements into great ones and made him sound like he could be applying for the Nobel Peace Prize or President of the United States. His resume was over the top for any job in our field.

Word to the wise… write your resume, solicit help for critical feedback—*"own" your resume.*

Three Types of Resumes

As you are probably aware, there are three types of resumes: (1) chronological; (2) functional; and (3) combination.

Chronological: This style is frequently used, when your work history has been stable, and your professional career has been consistent. This format follows your work history backward from your current job listing dates and accomplishments.

Note: *You should avoid this format, if frequent job changes have occurred, you have had negative performance issues, or have been demoted.*

Functional: This format is used by applicants who have been unemployed for long periods of time or have jumped around too frequently. It is written with the most relevant experience to the job you are seeking placed first and downplays employment dates, job titles, or district names.

Note: *In my opinion, this format does not work well for educational school leadership positions.*

Combination: This is my favorite layout and can be used when you have a steady or positive work history, with demonstrated accomplishments or if you happen to have subtle gaps in your employments history. This approach combines the chronological and functional resumes and begins with a brief summary statement.

Job specific skills, relevant to the position, are listed in a chronological format that lists the *how, when* and *where* skills were acquired. The reader can readily grasp a full picture of you as a leader working for them, within this format.

Note: *Try to use this format, if possible, when applying to positions of leadership in education.*

WINNING PLAYS FOR RESUMES

Tip #1: Use an impressive design that grabs attention:

A great resume is so pleasing to the eye that the reader is enticed to pick it up and read it. It stimulates interest and entices the reader to learn more about you. Employers make snap judgments, when skimming through your resume. The design must highlight the most important information about the applicant's work, experiences, skills, and education.

Tip #2: Create a tagline, stating your expertise:

"What's a *tagline?*" you ask. Taglines are also known as "objectives" and are commonly used by educators in their resumes. In my opinion, taglines that are written as objectives are out-of-style. Focus your tagline in a way that makes you stand out among other applicants.

Whether marketing a new business, chainsaws, doughnuts, or yourself, as a job candidate, the goal is to sell the product. In a job search, you are selling yourself in a very competitive market, to a very specific clientele. What is it that makes you stand out above your competition? Why are you a better candidate?

Here's an example of a tagline used in a superintendent resume:

- *Student focused leader with a strong record of success. Recognized for developing mutual trust and respect, building collaborative teams, public speaking, and sharing information through open communication.*

Here's another tagline used for a high school principal position:

- *Accomplished instructional leader known for being an energetic and caring professional. Proven record for building high functioning teams and working through sensitive issues with positive results. A collaborative decision maker and master working under pressure.*

Here's a different format for a tagline used on a superintendent resume:

> ## STRENGTHS:
>
> *Relationships* - Quickly established loyal and trusting relationships with key district stakeholders.
>
> *Raising Student Achievement* - Provided leadership for raising test scores in three school districts.
>
> *Revenue Enhancement* - Responsible for balanced budget ending with a 12% reserve, with no layoffs.

Tip #3: Create content that sells the benefit of your skills:

Cool resume design and killer taglines grab attention, but resume *content* is what finally sells the reader. Too many resumes that come across my desk list the person's job classification, followed by job duties. I advise my clients, "We all know what the role of an assistant principal entails—why are you telling us this?"

Rather, spend valuable white paper, telling the reader what you have done in your role to make a difference and why your performance is better than others. Go beyond showing what is required, and demonstrate how you make a difference. Provide specific examples. Ask yourself the following questions:

1. How do you perform better than others?
2. What are some problems or challenges faced and how did you overcome them?
3. Have you receive any awards or recognition as a result?

> **INSIDER TIP**
> Ways to use your resume:
>
> 1. Job application
> 2. Profile on LinkedIn or other job board
> 3. Copy on hand to refer to with phone conversations
> 4. Job fairs
> 5. Copies for all in-person interviews
> 6. Networking

Begin with your current position held, and then list recent accomplishments under each job.

Here are some examples that go beyond listing basic requirements of the job:

List your current district.	California School District (ADA 10,500)
Include brief address, enrollment, and job title.	Orange County, CA 92650 Superintendent
Title the next category.	Professional Accomplishments:
Now list accomplishments for each job you have held.	Successfully developed and monitored $100 million budget and produced a stabilization plan that enabled California Unified to end the school year with 18% reserve, gaining positive certification. District was applauded by the state for no layoffs or pay cuts.
List about 5-7 for your current position and 3-5 for each prior job.	Launched California Virtual High School to meet the needs of parents and students in the 21st century. This flexible district learning program provided all academic courses offered in a traditional setting, including CSU/UC approved A-G and AP courses.
Use quantifiable language to show success.	Established a successful Aspiring Administrators Symposium for 75 California School District teachers and authored corresponding article to promote success of the program (Leadership Magazine, September, 2006). Ten participants from the program were hired as administrators.

Here's another sample with examples of professional accomplishments:

Orange County Unified School District (ADA 15,000)
Orange County, California 92544
Superintendent

Professional Accomplishments:

- Created a One-Hundred Day Plan upon entry as superintendent. Conducted meetings to gather information for goal setting and to gain credibility in the community. Delivered Strategic Agenda to community upon completion.
- Managed and successfully monitored progress for the construction of a new high school, athletic complex, district transportation center and agricultural facility.
- Served as ex-officio member of the Citizens Bond Oversight Committee and District Master Plan for Facilities.
- Redesigned the hiring process for administrators and teachers to include community panels and performance assessments.
- Realized over $5.6 million in new 2011 revenue from transportation grants, Microsoft funding and E-Rate applications.
- Responsible for the passage of a $152 million general obligation bond supported by 64% of Orange County's citizens.
- Led the district initiative to develop user-friendly budgets within the context of transparent and all inclusive budget development processes.
- Led the process for implementation of a parent requested Voluntary Drug Testing Program for high school students.
- Responsible for the opening of OC High School, a community day school, serving expelled and high-risk youth.
- Implemented AVID at all middle schools, providing a seamless transition to a successful high school AVID Program.
- Delivered annual "State of the District" addresses in community forums, detailing progress made toward district goals.
- Led the process for a High School Quality Design Team, which met to engage in research-based high school reform efforts. Nine initiatives were charted as key areas of reform.

Tip #4: Use Power Words:

Tip #3 demonstrated that using numbers to quantify your achievements and responsibilities can elevate your image. This strategy creates a clear image, whereas general statements may not be easily quantifiable in the reader's mind. The more specific you are in describing accomplishments, the better off you are.

Another strategy to manage the image a prospective employer develops about you is to use "power words" to signify the position you want. Think about what jobs you are applying for… positions of management and leadership, right? Try to strengthen your image as an educational leader, by using as many "leadership" or "in charge" key words as possible.

Which example below do you think is the strongest?

Maintained oversight of a student attendance program.	Provided leadership for developing a student attendance program resulting in a 5% increase in student attendance over one year.

There are many articles on the internet about what not to write on a resume, what not to say, and words to avoid. I recently read "10 Buzzwords to Avoid on your Resume" and "Big Resume Blunders." The web is flooded with these tidbits, because our country is experiencing a huge unemployment crisis, and the competition for jobs is fierce.

You might take some comfort in the fact that, in the field of educational administration, the competition has always been fierce. As you know, we are a people-business and basically a teaching industry. We don't respond well to cutting edge, private sector thinking.

For example, do not be distracted when reading something on the internet that is stated like this: "Avoid the word *creative* on your resume. This word will turn off a person reading any job application."

I advise you not to give too much credence to the skyrocketing growth of professional networking sites. I just finished reading another article that suggested a candidate wrap their resume in fancy tissue paper to get attention. I doubt school people would embrace this technique. While some of the tips on the internet are good, remember, we use the word "creative" in our field, and we like that term. We haven't turned off on these words just yet, so don't be afraid to use them—and don't let internet hype make you change a resume that currently works for you!

Here is a list of power words you can use to build your resume.

POWER WORDS FOR RESUMES

Management Skills	Communication Skills	Clerical or Detailed Skills
administered	addressed	approved
analyzed	arbitrated	arranged
assigned	arranged	catalogued
attained	authored	classified
chaired	corresponded	collected
contracted	developed	compiled
consolidated	directed	dispatched
coordinated	drafted	executed
delegated	edited	generated
developed	enlisted	implemented
directed	formulated	inspected
evaluated	influenced	monitored
executed	interpreted	operated
improved	lectured	organized
increased	mediated	prepared
organized	moderated	organized
oversaw	motivated	prepared
planned	negotiated	processed
prioritized	persuaded	purchased
produced	promoted	recorded
recommended	publicized	retrieved
reviewed	reconciled	screened
scheduled	recruited	specified
strengthened	spoke	systematized
supervised	translated	tabulated
	wrote	validated

Research Skills	Technical Skills	Teaching Skills
clarified	assembled	adapted
collected	built	advised
critiqued	calculated	clarified
diagnosed	computed	coached
evaluated	designed	communicated
examined	devised	coordinated
extracted	engineered	developed
identified	fabricated	enabled
inspected	maintained	encouraged
interpreted	operated	evaluated
interviewed	overhauled	explained

investigated	programmed	facilitated
organized	remodeled	guided
reviewed	repair	informed
summarized	solved	initiated
surveyed	trained	instructed
systematized	upgraded	persuaded
		set goals
		stimulated

Financial skills	**Creative skills**	**Helping skills**
administered	acted	assessed
allocated	conceptualized	assisted
analyzed	created	clarified
appraised	designed	coached
audited	developed	counseled
balanced	directed	demonstrated
budgeted	established	diagnosed
calculated	fashioned	educated
computed	founded	expedited
developed	illustrated	facilitated
forecasted	instituted	familiarized
managed	integrated	guided
marketed	introduced	referred
planned	invented	rehabilitated
projected	originated	represented
researched	performed	
	planned	
	revitalized	
	shaped	

Boston College. 21, January 2012. Boston College Career Center Action Verbs
<http://www.bc.edu/offices/careers/skills/resumes/verbs.html>

Tip # 5: Include relevant professional information:

Structure your resume around headings relevant to our field, and then list information under each heading. Each category should have at least two listings.

Here are some workable headings with examples under each category:

TEACHING EXPERIENCE	PROFESSIONAL LEARNING
Long Beach Unified School District, CA 6-8 Math and Science	School Business Managers Academy ACSA Superintendents Academy
HONORS AND AWARDS	**PRESENTATIONS**
California School Administrator of the Year California Outstanding Administrator - John Hopkins University	CSBA Education Conference Building Leadership in the Middle School

PUBLICATIONS	COMMUNITY RELATIONS
Go to the Head of the Class	Orange County Educational Compact
The School Administrator, October 2009	California ROP Advisory Board
Superintendent Gets Taken for a Ride	Presidents' Commission on Teacher Education
The School Administrator, February 2009	

PROFESSIONAL AFFILIATIONS	REFERENCES
Association of California School	Dr. Richard Smith
Administrators	Bolder County Superintendent
American Association of School	760-330-5544
Administrators	

Tip #6: Identify and solve employer needs:

It is important to identify employer needs, by reading the job prospectus and then focusing your experience and skill set toward those areas on your resume. You can also research a school district, by studying their website.

Underline key areas of need, such as curriculum, high dropout rate, student achievement, finance, or team building. Also, contact people you know, who can share additional information about the job or school district.

Try to focus your resume on district concerns, if possible. For example, if the job advertisement lists, "Desirable Skills: Ability to reduce the student dropout rate," try to include something from your past experience about working with programs that address the dropout problem. Don't miss an opportunity to tie your expertise to district needs.

Tip #7: Prioritize the content of your resume:

Applicants often make the mistake of listing important data in the later parts of their resumes. As you compose headings for your resume, prioritize them by importance, impressiveness, and relevance to the job you want. For example, education is not always listed on the front page of a resume. However, if you attended Harvard, Stanford, or Princeton, it would make sense to list your educational achievements on page one, for greater impact. Get the point?

Tip #8: Avoid personal pronouns and articles:

A resume is a form of business communication, so it should be concise and written in a telegraphic style. There should be no mention of "I" or "me" and only minimal use of articles.

For example:

I developed a student attendance program that increased the district's daily rate of attendance from 96.1% to 98%.

Should be changed to:

Developed student attendance program that increased the district's daily rate of attendance from 96.1% to 98%.

Tip #9: Don't list irrelevant information:

Personal information, such as date of birth, marital status, hobbies should not be on an educational leadership resume.

Tip #10: Don't worry if your resume is too long or too short:

Don't worry about making your resume too long or too short. In an effort to squeeze their experiences onto one page, many applicants delete important information. There are no hard and fast rules governing appropriate resume length.

I submitted a concise and powerful, easy to read four-page resume, when applying for assistant superintendent and superintendent positions. These resumes always resulted in interviews, and no one ever indicated that my resume was too long. On the other hand, a teacher entering administration for the first time will not have enough experiences or accomplishments to warrant a four-page resume.

When writing your resume, it is important to ask yourself this question: "Will this statement help me win an interview?"

Tip #11: No typos!

One typo could result in your application being sent to the shredder. Educators are in the business of teaching children to read and write, and typos read like profanity in our profession. Have several colleagues and friends proofread your resume before submitting. This document is a reflection of your work and should be perfect.

WRITE ON!

> **INSIDER TIP**
> **Every Resume should contain:**
>
> - A heading that includes name, phone number, email and mailing address.
> - Some work history no matter how brief.
> - Education history.

Writing or revising one's resume can be a daunting task. Get a cup of coffee, set up your computer, and get to work. Follow these simple tricks of the trade to get you off the starting block:

1. Check out a few sample resume books to get ideas.

2. Pick a design template from Word or a similar program, or develop one on your own. Begin with your name and pertinent information at the top.

3. Arrange your categories in a fashion that makes sense to you, and prioritize according to their importance. Collate the important information within each category.

4. Write to your audience. How will your experience, skills and degrees fulfill the requirements of the new job? Show how your experiences from your last job will be valuable to the one you are applying for. If you are a teacher, try to showcase your leadership experience from the classroom, and align it to experience that would be desirable as an assistant principal.

   For example, avoid writing: "Worked with grade level teachers to develop a job fair." Turn your grade level experience into something more powerful, such as: "Provided leadership at the site level for our sixth grade job fair."

5. Now go back and edit. Tighten up your writing to keep it concise and action-oriented to focus on your accomplishments and responsibilities. You don't have to use complete sentences —bulleted lists are best.

6. Set your first draft down on a table, walk away for a few minutes, and then come back and glance at the front page. Does the formatting grab your attention, or is it just ho-hum? Think about formatting the document, so that it's graphically appealing. Do your headings jump out? Are fonts in synch? Work on this, until you feel you have a reader friendly document that is visually pleasing. Eliminate small type and long, rambling sentences.

7. Ask a few people to proofread, and then review it again yourself. Read each sentence in reverse for typos or words out of place.

8. Save your document in several places, and be prepared to tweak your resume to address the specific skills each school district requests.

Parting Shots

Congratulations—you're done! That wasn't difficult, was it? Now put on your thinking cap, sharpen a pencil, and let's move on to the next chapter: Preparation - Practice Makes Perfect. You will need to prepare for all the interviews you're going to get, as a result of the spectacular paperwork you just created!

Section IV:

PREPARATION - Practice Makes Perfect

"There are no secrets to success. It is the result of preparation, hard work, and learning from failure."
~ Colin Powell

Waiting for an invitation to interview, after all your hard work creating perfect paperwork, can be exasperating. Receiving a call to interview, however, is thrilling. For an instant, it feels like you've met your goal. Reality sets in quickly, however, when you realize that you've only completed the first step on your journey. Interviewing for a job involves a lot of work, research, preparation and practice! With so many hours writing a cover letter and resume, you don't want to perform poorly in the interview. That's where preparation and practice fit into our equation.

Game Time

When called to interview, make your response to the news positive and inquisitive. Try to sound excited that you have been selected to interview.

Say something like, "This is great news. I am excited to interview and learn more about the school district."

Listen first to what the caller has to offer, then use this opportunity to ask questions, if the information you need isn't provided.

Some questions to ask include:

1. What is the exact time to show up for the interview?
2. Where is the interview held?
3. What's involved? Are there one or two panels?

4. Is there a writing exercise? If so, ask if you can bring your own computer. Many times, a district doesn't mind, because applicants are more comfortable with their own technology. It depends—so don't forget to ask.

5. Who (not names—but job classification) is on the interview panel(s)?

6. What time span is involved? One-two hours?

7. How many candidates are being interviewed? Sometimes the district won't share this information, but if they do, it can be helpful to know how many people you are competing with.

8. What is the search timeline? Occasionally, the district will tell you the timeline, if they know the specifics. If you can't gain this information on this initial phone call, ask the search consultant the day of the interview.

9. Secure a phone number for the main contact person, in case something unexpected comes up the day of the interview— death in family, traffic accident, etc. Notice how bleak these circumstances sound? Call only in dire emergencies.

10. That's it. Don't ask about salary, chances for getting the job, or what kind of questions you may be asked. Your first responses are important, and if you ask inappropriate questions, it will be noted.

    Be cool, calm and collected. You can use this phone call to ask about the interview, but don't push too hard. The call should not take more than three to five minutes.

> **INSIDER TIP**
> When speaking on the phone to a district representative, smile when you speak. Putting that smile on your face ensures that you will present a positive phone image.

11. Try not to call back. Remember, it is important to be calm concerning the interview. You don't want to be labeled as a phone pest. Get all your information in one phone call, if possible.

Interviews—Up Close and Personal

Most school districts use a panel format to conduct initial interviews. After the paper screening, a select number of applicants are chosen for first-round interviews. This number can reach ten to fifteen and usually includes all "in-house" candidates. Many districts have an informal policy of granting interviews to current employees, as an opportunity to review and assess talent within their own district.

The majority of school districts conduct their initial interview in one day, but if a large pool of candidates exists, the sessions may continue into a second day. Interview panels are usually convened by the district office, and the composition varies across districts.

There is no set formula for panel compositions; however, the majority of districts try to select a wide range of participants. People selected to serve on an interview panel are considered gatekeepers for the school district and are often given the responsibility for final cuts. For example, a typical screening panel for a school principal will consist of several school principals, a handful of directors, an assistant superintendent and various support staff (i.e. school secretary, instructional assistant, and perhaps a union president). In addition, a cross section of teachers from the site opening may be asked to serve on the panel.

In my experience, these people are well liked and respected by top district administration and are known for being "team" players. They are also known for being highly dependable and not expected to deviate from the norm.

Why am I telling you this? Because, it is important to know that, while you may be an "out of the box" thinker or have some great ideas on how to change the face of education, the interview may not be the best place to share these thoughts. The interview panel has power over who is selected for final round interviews, and in some cases they may even decide upon a final candidate. Careful thought went into their selection for the panel, and it is important that you remember why.

The same holds true for panels consisting of search consultants and board of education members. They are elected by their community, and in the case of the search consultant, hired by the board, and as a rule are very conservative people. They are not known for being risk-takers and as a result often respond favorably to predictable and conservative candidates.

I am not suggesting that you change who you are, for the sake of gaining a new job. What I am suggesting is this. These people have the power to make or break you. Some may not be current on the latest educational research or philosophies. Some may even have personal axes to grind. So when applying for a new position, be aware of the political and emotional overtones you may encounter in your interview. Take note, and do what it takes to gain their acceptance (as long as you stay true to your own values)—and get hired.

Then, after taking a seat in your new administrative position, you can ease into new reform initiatives and perspectives about how schools should be run, if that is important to you. In my opinion, gatekeepers have kept schools running fairly constant and unchanged over the past century.

Have you ever wondered why it is that in many schools we place all ten-year-olds in one classroom, with one teacher, to learn a "one size fits all" curriculum? Times are very different now, and the face of education is dramatically changing. We need innovative and creative leaders in education. Our gatekeepers have a job to do, and you need to do what it takes to get hired. This is not the time to take a stand over an issue, share your thoughts about irresponsible parents, or sell a new program no one has ever heard of. Get promoted first!

Many districts form two separate panels—a district/technical panel and a community panel. The classification for these two panels can change, but basically, a community panel consists of parents, teachers, community partners, and support staff, while the district/technical panel consists of district senior management. A lead district administrator typically convenes the community panel and reports back their recommendations to the district/technical panel. The district panel then uses this information, in combination with their own results, to decide which candidates will move to finalist status.

When interviewing for a superintendent position, board of education members and the search consultant usually serve on the interview panel. Some boards will initially consider including key district stakeholders on these panels, but then change course, since confidentially issues come into play in the process. Hiring boards soon learn that quality candidates don't want to be exposed in their own districts. Many candidates know that, when boards open up the panel to outside stakeholders, their names tend to get out to everyone by the next workday.

One of my colleagues made the mistake of not telling his board that he was interviewing for a superintendent position in a district 200 miles away from his current district. He was assured by the search consultant that all members on the "community panel" had signed letters of confidentially and that he should not worry about the word getting back to anyone in his present district.

> **INSIDER TIP**
>
> If you don't want to advertise you are interviewing take a full or half-day off from work. If you have multiple interviews try to schedule them first thing in the morning or at the end of the day to reduce your loss of work.

He interviewed on a Friday afternoon and was stunned on Sunday evening, when he received an email from his teacher's union president that read, "I heard you're leaving us for another district."

As a result of this concern, many consultants are recommending a "board only" panel composition. In many states, however, superintendent candidates must be interviewed in open meeting forums, to comply with state law. In that case, the media will reveal the names of the finalists to the public. Pertinent questions should be asked in advance, regarding how to handle this issue.

Panel interviews can take thirty minutes to an hour. If a candidate is interviewing with two panels, they can expect to spend at least forty-five minutes with each panel. No matter how the interview is set up, you must work with the structure, to do your best.

Panel interviewers tend to have a set number of fixed questions that they ask each candidate. Sometimes, the lead interviewer conducting the search asks all the questions, and on occasion, each panel member will ask a question or two. The structure varies. I suggest that you not stress over the composition of the panel. Merely learn their status in the district, their job classification, if possible—and prepare for an outstanding performance!

During the interview, panel members are advised not to feed off an applicant's answers. The conventional question/answer format prevents this from happening, which is fortunate for the applicant, because answering unplanned questions on the fly can be a prescription for disaster.

Many times, applicants are given the questions in written form, which can help, as the questions are read aloud. If you are a candidate who needs eye glasses to read, you must now decide what to do with your glasses. Putting glasses on and off during an interview is distracting to a panel, so you must prepare how to deal with this concern.

Sometimes, candidates are given the questions fifteen to twenty minutes in advance of the interview. I always liked this format, because it gave me the opportunity to think through the technical aspects of a question. This approach helped to avoid "bird walking" on a question, during the interview. If you are afforded this opportunity, make simple bulleted notes in the margins next to each question, to guide you through the interview.

Initial cuts are typically made immediately after the interviews, and those remaining are called "finalists." Finalists are called and instructed to meet with senior staff, the superintendent, or conceivably, a board member. Districts like to call these final rounds "meetings," but don't be fooled—this is another interview in disguise. While they appear more informal than first round interviews, I like to think of these meetings as "elimination interviews."

Finalists are usually top candidates, and by the time one gets to the finals, it's more about *elimination* rather than *selection*. Final round panel members tend to like all the finalists and have a difficult time eliminating candidates they really like. So, if you are fortunate enough to make a final round, consider yourself in fairly good shape with your interviewing skills.

Extra Credit

Many school districts like to include performance tests in the interview process. These can include writing exercises, budget dissections or impromptu oral presentations. These tasks require you to be "cool under fire."

You will sit in a room to prepare, usually someone's office. Don't touch any of the items on the desk, unless instructed to do so. When using a district computer, remember to save your work every few minutes. You will most likely be given a time limit, and you don't want your work to be lost on a computer you are not familiar with.

While writing under pressure isn't the best situation, do your best, and stick to the prompt. Don't stress out, if you are not a great writer. Write in complete sentences, stay on topic, and review for typos (don't forget spellcheck).

Sometimes applicants are asked to hand write the assignment on a legal pad, which may be insulting for tech-savvy individuals. Again, be cool, and avoid sharing your frustration by saying something like… "No computers?" Perform as well as possible on the exercise, and make sure your handwriting is legible.

As an aside, I have rarely seen performance exercises used as a basis to exclude candidates. Occasionally, in the interest of time, panels neglect to even review them. The best advice is to watch the clock, and do your best. Do not complain or apologize to the secretary who collects your work, by saying, "I could have done better with my own computer," or "I don't have real good handwriting," or "Timelines make me nervous." Again, show your professionalism to all personnel—and stay cool under pressure.

Dress for Success

Entire books have been devoted to the subject of interview attire. I wrote a chapter on the subject in my book for women gaining access to top leadership positions, entitled, *The SeXX Factor: Breaking the Unwritten Codes that Sabotage Personal and Professional Lives*. I have concluded that one should not perseverate on this issue. Simply dress for the job.

Administrators, on their best days, wear suits and ties. Show that you fit in, by wearing clothes to an interview that send the right message. Members of the interview panel should think that you look like an administrator.

> **INSIDER TIP**
> Wear clothing that signifies leadership and success. Don't wear a new fad or style to an interview such as a fur scarf or animal print.

A few years ago, many believed the "interview outfit" was a deal breaker for being hired. There were actually codes written in self-help books that said women should not wear pants, and men should not wear black suits to an interview.

RULES OF THE GAME

Things have changed, and people now have a more casual attitude toward dress in the workplace. It would be a mistake, however, to underdress for the occasion.

Here are some common sense tips regarding interview attire for an administrative position in a school district:

- If you are interviewing for a leadership position *wear a suit.* Teachers often reveal they do not own a suit. I strongly recommend that they borrow one, or purchase an inexpensive suit at a discount store for interviewing. Teachers need to look like an administrator, when applying for leadership positions.

- Women can wear pants or dress suits but should *not* wear a red or "Easter egg" colored suit. Avoid distracting jewelry (less is more), long flashy fingernails, over the top make-up, perfume, or frilly suits. *Sandals should not be worn.*

- If you are overweight, make sure your suit jacket has enough room throughout. A jacket worn too tight across the arms and back may suggest to some interviewers that the applicant is carrying too much weight. Concerns over health and job performance may arise. Panels want to hire *healthy, energetic* administrators, who can manage long work days. If you are overweight, seek out a professional wardrobe consultant to help you select clothing that will counteract any possible negative perceptions.

- Men should *wear a suit and tie*—with no exceptions. I'll go on record, however for breaking the "no exception" rule.

As a superintendent, I sat on a panel to hire a high school principal. After interviewing ten candidates, I was struck by a gentleman wearing a leather sweater jacket, or something to that affect. Throughout his interview, I was distracted by his jacket. Not only was it strange looking, but I couldn't recall any principals I had ever known wearing something like this to work.

The reason I am mentioning this story is because the man was absolutely a fantastic candidate. I wanted to hire him about midway through the interview. He delivered exceptional answers, came highly recommended, and had some great ideas about how to turn the high school around. Everyone on the panel placed him in the top two, and he advanced to the final round.

While I was confident he would be an exceptional high school principal, his jacket kept nagging at me: "What kind of a man misses the mark like this?" I thought. If he could wear a strange looking jacket to an interview—what would he wear to Back to School night?

I was very relieved in the final interview, when he wore a regular suit and tie. We have become good friends over the years, and I have mentored this man to reach his goal of becoming a superintendent. I reminded him to leave his sweater jacket "back at the ranch."

Case in point: *Don't create doubt in an employer's mind by wearing inappropriate attire to an interview.*

- As a woman, you will most likely carry a purse, which should not present a problem. Some women applicants ask the receptionist to hold their purse, just before going into an interview. At an interview for a superintendent position, a search consultant once grabbed my purse and placed it in the back of the interview room, which disturbed my concentration and put me off. Some women choose to leave their purse in the car, but since most applicants carry a comb and makeup, they need these backup tools before interviewing.

  I recommend you *keep your purse near you, during the interview.* In addition, your purse should be *professional*, rather than a fashion showstopper. Walk in the room, take a seat, and place your purse on the floor next to your chair.

- Whatever you choose to wear, *you must feel comfortable.* It is important to get used to wearing the whole outfit, while standing, sitting, and walking—*and never wear a newly purchased suit for the first time to an interview.*

Never Fear

As expressed previously in this book, my first interview for an administrative position was a prescription for disaster. With preparation, however, came confidence, and I actually started to like the interview process.

All athletes know that the increased stress of competition often causes them to respond, both physically and mentally, in a manner that negatively affects their performance. This stress often causes nervousness, increased heart rates, and breaking into cold sweats. As a result, athletes worry about the outcome of the competition, and find it hard to concentrate on the task in hand.[4]

An increasing interest in the field of sports psychology—and in particular, in the area of competitive anxiety—have resulted in the development of techniques that athletes use in competitive situations, to maintain control and optimize their performance. Once learned, these techniques allow the athlete to relax and to focus his/her attention in a positive manner on the task of preparing for and participating in competition.

One of these techniques is known as pre-visualization or mental imaging. Basically, the athlete sets the state for their performance, with a complete mental run-through of the key elements of their performance. Mental imagery does not focus on the outcome but rather on the actions to achieve the desired outcome.

Golfer Jack Nicklaus used mental imagery for every shot. In describing how he imagines his performance, he wrote:

I never hit a shot even in practice without having a sharp in-focus picture of it in my head. It's like a color movie. First, I "see" the ball where I want it to finish, nice and white and sitting up high on the bright green grass. Then the scene quickly changes, and I "see" the ball going there: its path, trajectory, and shape, even its behavior on landing. Then there's a sort of fade-out, and the next scene shows me making the kind of swing that will turn the previous images into reality and only at the end of this short private Hollywood spectacular do I select a club and step up to the ball.[5]

Interviewing for a new job is much like competing for a high stakes athletic competition. With that metaphor in mind, I used a simple technique every time I interviewed for a position, which helped to alleviate some of my nervousness. On the following page is a snapshot of my interview preparation—keeping the pre-visualizing technique in mind.

[4]Brian Mac Sports Coach, "Psychology, January 2012.
<http://www.brianmac.co.uk/psych.htm>

[5]Crossfit Vancouver, School of Fitness. 20, January 2012.

Before every interview, I review my interview notes, run a mile in the morning, eat a respectable breakfast or lunch, and prepare my wardrobe, and make up for my interview. As soon as I arrive at the district office, I immediately try to find a women's room.

Once there, I adjust my hair and make-up, and smile into the mirror, and begin to tell myself positive affirmations. Then I close my eyes, and attempt to visualize myself sitting at a table, looking comfortable and confident. I see panel members nodding their heads in agreement, as I deliver stunning answers to challenging questions. Everyone is smiling, including me.

Pleased with the pre-visualization exercise, I assertively look into the mirror and say to myself, "Go strong." I walk out of the restroom, smiling and ready to take on the world.

Many people become nervous and fearful before and during a job interview. This feeling is a normal response to the pressure to do well and impress the people interviewing you. The anxiety is very similar to that experienced in public speaking and can be easily conquered with practice.

To be self-assured in an interview greatly enhances your chances to be hired, while being fearful and uncertain increases your odds of failure. Prepare for the interview in the same way you would for a public speech. *Preparation is invaluable.* You need to have an arsenal of examples, stories and threads to call upon during the interview, which will help project an image of self-confidence.

When I make reference to threads, I don't mean you must study or memorize answers to every conceivable question that could possibly be asked in a job interview. Rather, I propose that applicants should integrate key strands that coincide with educational themes, that will most likely arise in an interview. We'll work on these themes a bit later in this chapter.

Behind Closed Doors

What do panels look for during an interview? Simply put, they will look for evidence that will help them construct an image of what kind of an employee you will make. It's safe to assume that, since you were invited to the interview, you have already met certain qualifications expected in the position. It's a given the panel has met in advance, to prepare for their part in the interview process. The questions they have discussed and finessed are geared to determine if you:

1. Can do the job (expertise and ability)
2. Want to do the job (willingness and team spirit)
3. Are fun or dreadful to work with (do we like you?)

And that's about it. Everything you say and do in the interview revolves around your talent, character, and likability, and it will be highly scrutinized by the interviewers who are, in most cases, people you don't know.

First Impressions

Research suggests that the impressions created in the first few minutes of the interview are the most lasting. I've read that an interview panel decides if they like you, within the first twenty seconds of meeting you. That sounds a little extreme, to me. While making a good first impression is important, I believe that a lot happens throughout the course of an interview. I don't think too many panels select a final candidate, within the first twenty seconds. However, there are a few torpedoes that can sink any applicant:[6]

Sick to Death: No one wants to be ill on this important day, but if you have the flu, a fever, can't get out of bed or vomiting—you can't be a martyr and show up. The employer doesn't want to risk getting the flu. But if you can possibly make it, that's another matter.

In our field, be aware that it is rare to get a second chance to interview, if you call in sick. I'm sorry to be the messenger of bad news, but educators are very rigid people and aren't known for changing schedules made in advance (think rainy day schedules). If you can physically endure the interview, go for it, but do not—I repeat, *do not*—apologize for being sick, or divulge your illness. If you do—*you lose.* Panel members will not appreciate being put in harm's way and will shy away from you during the interview.

---

[6]Areas suggested from: Wetfeet. **Twelve Ways to Make a Bad First Impression, January 2012.** <http://www.wetfeet.com/advice-tools/interviewing/12-ways-to-make-a-bad-first-impressionand-how-to-recover>

I recall one candidate blowing his nose, coughing, sneezing. He was real sick. We gave one another a glance and couldn't wait until he left the room.

Sticks and Stones: If you're hurt in some way—whether you have a bruised face, broken leg, or visible stitches—you may want to call ahead and explain your condition, especially if you need handicap access. If you decide not to call in advance, prepare to have a good story, regarding your black eye.

One day, a principal candidate walked into the interview room with bandages and crutches. She took ten minutes to sit down, and everyone felt her pain. She amused us, as she shared details about her Colorado skiing accident, in which a famous movie star drove her to the hospital.

Better late, than never? There is *no excuse for being late* to an interview. Mapquest your route in advance, and *arrive early*, if possible. If you are late, for some unforeseen reason that you haven't prepared for, call the interviewer, explain the situation, and ask if they still have time for you or if you can reschedule. It's not likely you will get a second chance, unless you are fortunate enough to get a sympathetic person on the other end of the phone. Rescheduled appointments are very rare.

Early Bird: Most districts tell you to arrive fifteen minutes in advance of your interview and are very explicit about it. Checking in too early with the receptionist and hanging out in the lobby before a scheduled appointment gives the impression you're desperate. If you arrive early, wait in a coffee shop, or just sit in your car. *Do not go into the office before your scheduled time.*

Idle Chatter: Making good use of your lobby time before your appointment is important. The secretary, receptionist, or janitor at work in the corner make opinions about you and are eager to share their first impressions. I have often been the beneficiary of such handed down conversations. *Don't engage in irrelevant conversation or play with your IPhone.* Use this time to your advantage, by discussing district information with the receptionist, studying the bulletin board, or reading available district brochures.

I recall an interview for a superintendent position, in which I sat in the lobby and talked with the main receptionist. During our conversation, she revealed that she was the superintendent's executive secretary. We talked about students, the new building, and the district's newspaper, proudly displayed on her desk.

This "interview receptionist" later turned out to be my secretary, since I was hired as the new superintendent. After one week on the job, she informed me that three board members approached her after my interview, wanting to know what she thought of me. She was eager to tell me that she had told each board member that I was the friendliest of all the applicants and that she would like to work with me. *Don't waste your lobby time.*

Sorry Handshake: If you offer either a limp or iron grip handshake, plan on making a less than positive first impression. Your handshake should signal friendliness and trustworthiness. *The ideal handshake creates a lasting first impression.*

Make sure your hands are clean and reasonably free from perspiration. To reduce sweaty palms, run them under cold water, or place them on your cheeks a few seconds, before the interview. Offering a limp hand gives the impression you're hesitant or meek. Giving a bone-crunching squeeze may give an impression of a domineering personality—and it can hurt! When you shake hands with a medium-firm grip, confidence and authority are conveyed. Also, *look your interviewer in the eye and say his or her name,* to make a confident, lasting impression.

Small Talk: When meeting the lead interviewer, be prepared with two or three things to say, to get the person talking. Be the first to say "Hello," and offer your handshake and name, to ease the pressure.

For example, *"Richard Smith? Marilou Ryder—a pleasure to meet you."* Then begin some small talk about the district's new building, displayed student photos, etc. By showing interest in their school district, you create synergy between you and the interviewer, and hopefully establish a connection.

Stranger than fiction: I once had a job candidate, who knew nothing about our district and pronounced the school's name wrong. Another applicant thought the superintendent had been recently fired and asked why. *Do your research, before the interview.* You don't have to know every small detail about the district, but don't blunder the big ones.

In addition, visiting the school district before an interview can be extremely beneficial. Not only will you learn about cost of living details, but you will also gain valuable information to use in the interview. Before interviewing, I always visited the school community and spent time asking students and parents what they thought about the school district. During interviews, I would make reference to the information gained from my informal conversations with community stakeholders. Panel members were always appreciative and impressed that I cared enough to visit their school district to learn about them.

Nice Recovery: No matter what goes wrong during your introduction—you can recover. It's *how* you recover that's important. In fact, reacting gracefully and showing calmness under pressure always impresses a panel.

I recall an applicant who hit the water bottle with her arm, as she sat down. Water went everywhere. The applicant knew how to recover, as she walked over to the snack table, picked up some napkins, wiped up the water and made us all laugh, as she poked fun of herself. She used the accident as an ice breaker. The good news for her was that she got the job.

Taking the Hot Seat

Once you enter the interview room, the lead interviewer will point to the "hot seat." Everyone calls it the hot seat, since they know interviewing can be a lot like "getting grilled."

Before sitting, some applicants use this opportunity to walk around the table, to individually greet and shake each member's hand. Please note—taking on this challenge in a small conference room can work to your disadvantage, so be careful when attempting this maneuver. It can be awkward, and you may want to pass on the opportunity. *Follow the lead's direction,* since it's not uncommon for the lead to seat you, and then ask each panel member to introduce themselves. After each member speaks, acknowledge them, by nodding your head and saying, "Nice to meet you," or "Hello."

Now you are really settled in, and the interview finally begins. After some small talk among panel members, a stillness will come over the room, and all eyes will be on *you*. Don't underestimate the importance of your posture and subtle movements. To ensure your body language signals confidence, sit up straight, with your shoulders back. Avoid crossing your legs, and don't act too casual in your approach. Even if you're nervous, try not to fidget. Don't play with your jewelry, twirl your hair or cross your arms—and try to maintain eye contact with the lead interviewer.

Play Ball: Question Number #1

Before or just after the first question is asked, take a moment to thank the panel. It can sound something like this:

I would like to take this opportunity to thank you for granting me an interview today. I am happy to be here and look forward to getting to know you better. Thank you.

This short exchange eases the transition between you sitting there and the onslaught of questions headed your way. It also affords you the opportunity to catch your breath and gain your composure. *Don't forget this important strategy.*

The first question, standard in the industry, takes a variety of forms but is designed to determine why you want the job, who you are, and why you think you're right for the position. That's a lot to ask in one question. This question doesn't vary much from assistant principal to superintendent, so it pays to prepare your answer in advance.

> **INSIDER TIP**
>
> Practice interviewing in front of the mirror or with a friend and treat your mock interview seriously. Practicing helps to control nervousness and increases confidence. Videotape yourself while you are rehearsing some of your stories. Review the tape for body language, and engagement. Learn to lean forward, smile and uncross your legs.

Practice your response, over and over, in front of a mirror and with friends, until you feel comfortable with what you are saying. Don't memorize your answer, but learn how to navigate through this first question. It's not an invitation to ramble, nor is it time to recite your resume.

Don't take off on where you went to grad school, or repeat your employment history. Panel members have read your resume and want more details from this question.

Whatever direction you choose to take, make sure your opening statement has relevance to the world of education. The tale you tell should demonstrate, or refer to, one or more of your key behavioral profiles in action—perhaps integrity, being a team player, or determination.

You may describe yourself as someone who is adept at communicating. If so, give an example from your current job that indicates your success:

> *For example, in my current role as principal, I am known for being an honest and open communicator. I believe that two-way communication establishes trust and creates the gateway for collaboration.*

When asked why you want to work for their school district, your research will come in handy, as you profess the district has an excellent reputation, and you believe the district would be a good match for your skill set. It's important to explain that you are not interested in merely getting a new job; rather, you are looking for a new challenge in your profession to work with students and make a difference. The first question allows you to share that their district's values align with yours, enabling you to fit in and complement their team.

The first question is not one that can be answered effectively off the cuff. *I strongly advise you to take time in advance*, and think about yourself and key aspects of your personality and/or background that you want to promote or feature, during this critical opening question. This is your time to shine, and make a positive first impression. Practice, by completing the following sample exercise on the following page.

INSIDER TIP

Avoid personal opinion in an interview. Instead of saying, "I believe my program reduced truancy," rely on someone else's opinion such as, "My superintendent reports that the program I recently developed reduced truancy by 10%.

Tell us about yourself: List three personal qualities you bring to the job—and back each one up with *evidence*:

   1. People Person

   2.

   3.

Quality #1: People Person

<u>Evidence</u>: *I like to communicate openly with all stakeholders, build teams, and I have a great sense of humor.*

Quality #2:
<u>Evidence</u>:

Quality #3:
<u>Evidence</u>:

Qualifications and skills you bring to position: List three qualifications or skills—and back each one up with *evidence*:

   1. Excellent Planning Skills

   2.

   3.

Skill #1: Excellent Planning Skills

<u>Evidence</u>: *Known for being an excellent planner. Recently developed a five year technology plan.*

Skill #2:
<u>Evidence</u>:

Skill #3:
<u>Evidence</u>:

Why you want to work there: Develop a story about why you want the job or desire to work with the district.

<u>Example</u>: *Your school district has developed a long term goal of increasing student achievement for all students. I have read your instructional action plan and believe my skills in planning and instruction can make a positive difference for students and impact the success of your plan.*

Game Time: The Interview

Now the panel gets to the heart and soul of the interview and asks a series of questions to determine your personality, decision making abilities, integrity, communication skills—and the list goes on. If you were a bit nervous during your opening statement, don't worry; ninety-nine percent of all applicants recover from being nervous, once the barrage of questions begins.

During the next phase of the interview, *your task is to get these people to like you.* You want to present yourself as a friendly person; someone they would like to have on their team. Smiling and sharing a heartfelt short story along the line helps. Listen carefully to each question, and if you don't understand something, ask to have it repeated or request clarification.

Many people in interviews talk too much and lose the sense of time. Keep each answer to less than three minutes, and don't ramble. Listen carefully to what is being said, and try not to be overly anxious to impress. Just answer each question to the best of your ability. Don't worry if you think you don't have the "right" answers.

One of my biggest "ah-ha's" learned over time is this: *There are no "right" or "wrong" answers in an interview.* There are just various degrees of good and bad responses.

> **INSIDER TIP**
>
> A good portion of interview prep should include verbally practicing your responses. Having information in your mind and articulating that information through speech are two very different activities.

Listening will allow you to answer the questions better and not cause panel members to think you've lost your way.

If you are asked a question that renders you speechless, pause and try to collect yourself. Whatever you do, don't plead stupidity or point out any of your personal weaknesses. Tell the panel you have no experience or knowledge in that area but are a fast learner and know how to find the information to address that issue.

Random Acts of Paperwork

I mentored a client, whose aspirations were to become an assistant superintendent. He was awarded several interviews, as a result of good experience and stellar paperwork but could not figure out why he continued to place second in most interviews. He confessed his thoughts of giving up his job search but still wanted one more chance to win.

We spent an hour over coffee, analyzing what a typical interview looked like, from his point of view. After hearing how he answered a few questions, I was somewhat perplexed. His resume was exceptional, he spoke well, and he possessed a depth of experience. I would have hired him in a minute. I probed a bit more and soon learned he was carrying a portfolio into his interviews.

"A portfolio," I prodded. "What does it look like?"

"I happen to have it right here," he exclaimed and proudly produced a fifty pound dossier; a black leather bound case, holding hundreds of photos, newspaper clippings, newsletters, strategic plans, letters from students, parents, awards—you name it, he had it all.

"How do you manage this in an interview?" I queried.

Somewhat annoyed and a bit offended, he said, "Well each time a question is asked, I pull out a few of my examples, talk about them, and then pass them around the table for everyone to share. They love it!"

I told him that I didn't think this tactic was his ticket to a promotion. Senior administrators serving on panels aren't real fans of portfolios in interviews. Some interviewers actually think they are a distraction. They want to hear from the applicant—not see photos.

I grabbed one from his binder. He was wearing a gold crown, sitting among students in a limousine. He looked at the photo and admitted he might be using the portfolio as a crutch, so he wouldn't have to be "on" for each question. I encouraged him to leave the portfolio home. He winced and didn't think it possible but said he'd give it a try.

"After all," he said, "I am paying you for advice, and I should listen." Two weeks later, he called to inform me he had accepted a new position and was very proud. "I got the job, without my security blanket," he exclaimed.

It is advisable, however, to bring a few simple samples of your work, as a backup. You may not need the material, but if there is a question you can't answer, you can refer to the material. (Make it a one-pager, and leave behind enough copies for everyone.)

Also, have your resume handy for reference and to distribute, if necessary. Having this material with you acts as a safety net, in case you have concerns about omitting something.

> **INSIDER TIP**
>
> Prepare real anecdotes, examples, results, and challenges from your previous work that you would like to mention. Memorize important data, years, etc. Practice telling your stories beforehand and make sure each one illustrates a skill or alludes to a quality character trait.

Don't bring a portfolio to an interview. It's distracting and presents problems for the lead interviewer and panel members. They want to listen and observe.

Going into Overtime

Okay, you've answered the questions, feel confident, and sense the panel likes you. Now, with only a few minutes remaining, someone will ask if you have any final comments or questions to ask the panel. This is your golden opportunity. You have a chance to make a lasting impression. Here are a few suggestions to maximize this critical moment:

- When asking questions, don't ask difficult questions or use it as an advantage to gain more face time. As a superintendent, I disliked it when an applicant asked me technical questions that made me feel like the interviewee. Ask questions that demonstrate your own values and work ethic, such as, "Does collaboration play a big part in your work style here?" Or specifically ask the lead interviewer why he likes working in the school district.

- Don't ask about salary, health benefits or number of sick days. You can, however, ask about the interview process and it is perfectly acceptable to request clarification regarding next steps and when to expect to hear from them.

- Finally and most importantly, thank them for their time and opportunity to get to know them better. Have a statement prepared in your mind to let them know you want the job and that you will be a valuable and collaborative member of their management team. Make your final statement brief and to the point then get up from your chair and shake hands with everyone.

First Things First

When the interview is over, get to your car and write down the questions you were asked. You may need these for the next interview. Take notes, and make sure you write down the names and titles of the key interview people. If the district asked for references during or after the interview, contact your references immediately, to notify them that they may soon be hearing from a prospective employer. If necessary, remind your references about some of your important traits or accomplishments.

As a superintendent, I never received a note of thanks from an applicant who had interviewed for a leadership position. Also, as an applicant, I never wrote a thank you note. The timeline for the hiring process is short, and finalists are often notified the same or next day. Some candidates reveal they write thank you cards in the car and bring them back into the district office and request that they be distributed to the panel. I believe this tactic is a little excessive.

No News is Good News—Right?

I am sorry to report there are districts that don't have good manners, when it comes to informing applicants of their status after an interview. This oversight always angered me, both as an applicant and as a superintendent. If you don't hear back, it's perfectly okay to check in on the status of your candidacy, within the time frame you were given. Call or email the lead interviewer, and thank them again, and restate your interest in the position. If you can't get connected with this person or don't hear back after your first follow-up or voice mail, you're not likely to hear back about the job. It's time to move on with your job search.

Stiff Upper Lip

If you are contacted by a district representative, informing you that you are not a finalist, try to stay poised. Thank the person for their time and consideration, and then ask if the school district honors follow up conferences for interview feedback. Assure the caller you truly appreciate an honest analysis, to learn why you weren't chosen for the position. If they agree to the conference, schedule an appointment as soon as possible. Our business is education, and the majority of assistant superintendents of human resources grant conference requests of this nature.

If you have interviewed in only one district, the rejection can be devastating. I encourage applicants to apply to as many positions as possible in their search. Rejection is difficult, but you should know that the competition for these top level positions is fierce. Rejection is part of the overall process, and not everyone can be right for every job.

Elimination from a candidate pool can be attributed to several variables, some which you can work on and some over which you have no control:

- The "in-house" candidate was a shoe in. The potential for an "in-house" candidate to secure a promotion is always present. Insiders have knowledge about the job and how the district functions. Many times they are encouraged to apply by their superintendents.

    "Why would a district put others through a grueling application and interview process?" you ask. Simple—to make an assessment of the talent readily available to them. It doesn't seem fair, but outside candidates often apply back to the same district at another time, often landing the job.

- You demonstrated lack of experience, lackluster recommendations or lacked effective interview skills. Unfortunately, most candidates who experience rejection fall into one of these areas. It is critical to find out which area pertains to you. Ask a mentor or colleague to help you determine any shortcomings.

- You're not a good match for the district. The ability to convince an interview panel you are a good match for their district can be challenging.

    You must be "yourself" in an interview. If you try to be someone you're not, they will sense it. Remember when you were dating a person you really liked a lot but just didn't feel the love. Interviewing is a lot like dating. A panel may like you and what you have to say in the interview—they just don't want to marry you. They think you have talent, knowledge, and initiative, but for some reason, they decide not to settle down with you. It's often hard to pin down, but that's how it works. A panel's work involves eliminating candidates from the field and selecting those to move on to finalist status.

They Like Me—They Really like Me!

Good news comes in two forms: (1) you're a finalist; or (2) we're giving you the position. Each one is a victory. One, of course, is sweeter than the other.

Being selected as a finalist means you are about to participate in more interviews. These interviews can take a variety of forms, from meeting alone with the superintendent and cabinet members to meeting with the Board of Trustees. These interviews tend to be more like a conversation. Follow the same format and interviewing techniques demonstrated during your initial interview, with a few exceptions.

As a finalist, hone in on the district, and be able to articulate how hiring you can positively impact their goals. A thorough research and discovery of how your skills align with their needs is important. Also, during these close quarter interviews, listen very carefully, not only to answer questions properly, but to determine if you actually want to work in the district.

You know you want the job—but let's be real. In applying for the job, you have learned about the district. What if working for a district means working for Attila the Hun or that you will be associated with a manager who fires everyone on a whim? This is your opportunity to determine if *they* are a good match for *you.*

Count Your Blessings

I recall a time when I was recruited for a superintendent position. I really wanted this job. The district was in a great location, had good test scores, a balanced budget, and a remarkable salary. I worked with a search firm who indicated the board of trustees was very interested in me and that, basically, this job was made for me. I was excited!

This particular search firm had a policy of completing the entire interview process in one day. They informed me after the first interview to stay close for a phone call, to alert me if I was selected as a finalist. I was at a coffee shop about a mile away, when two hours later, I received the call indicating the board "loved me" and just wanted to ask a few more questions.

As a result of rush hour, it took a little longer to get back to the district office. When I arrived for the final interview, the search consultant said the board was getting a little antsy waiting for my arrival. He explained that many of them wanted to "wind this up," as they expressed the need to get home for the holiday. When I entered the board room, I immediately became aware of some tension and sensed they were aggravated they had to wait for me.

Two board members began asking very technical and personal questions in rapid succession. One woman wanted to know how many sick days I took in my current position, and another inquired about how I used vacation days. Another actually asked me how many hours I worked per day.

I began to get a queasy feeling in my stomach, and then, in the middle of this confusing situation, I was overcome with clarity. I knew I did not want to work for this board who, in my opinion, were unnecessarily hostile. I knew that if I accepted the position, our relationship would at best be strained. I imagined that if they could get so upset over a few minutes of wait time—what would their behavior be like during board meetings?

I would not advise you to accept a job, just for the sake of winning. Use your final interview as an opportunity to discover if the job is right for you.

THE JOB OFFER

If you are called and offered the position, you will no doubt be excited. You should *sound* excited, even if you have some reservations about salary or some other aspect of the position. There are many different scenarios that can occur, once a job is offered. Here are a few to think about:

Sign Me Up

This scenario is the easiest of all and the one the employer usually wants. They are invested in the process and have much on the line. They have conducted interview sessions, brought key stakeholders together, checked references, and probably even tested the waters about your hire with important people (board of trustees, union presidents, etc.)

When the district calls and reports you are "the" candidate, you will be exuberant and, barring any conditions, you will tell the person calling that you are excited to accept the position. The district representative will share details about board approval, contracts, salary, and schedule an appointment for you to meet with human resources and payroll. In my experience, over ninety-five percent of all jobs offered in the field of educational administration go down this way—positive, quick and easy.

On the Fence

Some candidates, however, when offered a job, want to think about it. They may request one or two days, or even longer, for this process. They may have another offer in the works, another interview scheduled or want time to consider the offer. Many candidates worry, however, that the position might be offered to another candidate. The way you should play this out is dependent on your risk-taking abilities.

I'm reminded of an interview for an assistant superintendent position. I decided to hire a particular candidate but also liked the runner up. It had been a close call. I was excited to call the winning candidate, to congratulate her and hear her excitement. This did not happen. I hardly finished the good news, when she hesitated and said she had to think it over, because she didn't think the salary offered was commensurate with her experience.

When an offer is made, most districts consider it a professional courtesy to allow people a few days to think it over. I was shocked, because I thought this person really wanted to work with us. She played the "salary" card but knew I had to wait for her next move. I started to feel as if I had made a mistake and secretly hoped she wouldn't take the job, so I could move on to the runner up. Fortunately, she called back the next day to inform us she was taking a job elsewhere.

If you take time to think a job offer over, you are putting the district on hold. If you then decide to take the job, it can take some time to resolve some resentment. Remember, your career involves establishing long-term relationships. The hiring executive you impress may want to hire you several years from now, even if you don't accept the job offered today. Maintaining positive relationships within this high stakes arena is very important.

Walking a Tight Rope

Some candidates try to balance job offers with upcoming interviews. If this is your case, know that school districts are often under pressure to fill their positions. Delaying them to balance two or three job offers at once can work against you. There is no set etiquette for handling multiple offers, but the safe route is to inform each district of your additional offers. If you are their top candidate, they need to know of this activity.

If the school district wants to hold your feet to the fire regarding your decision, then you need to work on making your decision as soon as possible. These situations call for honesty and open communication, while trying not to muddle things in process. It is reasonable to ask for five days to formally accept an offer, but do not rush, if you aren't confident with a particular school district. Leverage your best interests for the long term.

For example, on rare occasions, competing school districts will accelerate their hiring pace, if they know they could lose a good candidate. However, as a candidate, you are unlikely to speed up the hiring process, just because it is a process. By that, I mean you are not the only candidate in the pool, and school districts are required to establish a hiring process that gives all qualified candidates equal access to the position.

There are no set solutions to these situations, and it's worth picking up the phone to ask a mentor or colleague to listen to your situation, and offer constructive feedback. It's hard to navigate all the variables on your own.

Negotiating Salary and Contract

Most jobs in educational leadership have a set salary schedule. When accepting a position, you will be asked to meet with human resources representatives. Someone in this department will place you on the salary schedule. A general rule of thumb for districts is to place new administrative hires on the schedule at a higher salary than they are currently making.

Districts are not so flexible, however, with health and welfare benefits. If your current district pays one hundred percent of your health insurance, and your new district charges employees $250 per month, as part of a cap, there won't be much negotiation. Health benefits are usually part of the collective bargaining agreement and are standard for all employees across the board. As a result, it pays to do your homework in advance, and research the range of pay for each position and whether health benefits have an employee contribution.

When teachers move from teacher status to administration, they are often amazed at the salary discrepancy. Teachers work on a set salary schedule and are often coaches, mentors, department chairs, or athletic/activity directors, resulting in additional salary stipends. It is not unusual for a teacher to make more than an assistant principal. Districts are aware of this and often work with candidates to place them on a salary schedule, to match or exceed what the teacher made before the promotion to assistant principal.

I advise teachers that, while in the short run moving to administration may not significantly increase their pay, they should consider this career move as an investment in their economic future.

The rules change quite a bit for superintendents. Most work under employment contracts, which are governed by state and federal statutes. As a new superintendent, you will probably be unfamiliar with the process and will need to ask for help with contract language, as well as strategies for negotiating with the board of trustees. Since quick turnaround time is the greatest challenge in this situation, it pays —*literally*—to hire an expert to help you navigate the negotiation process.

During my first superintendency, I made the mistake most new superintendents make. The board and their attorneys were eager for me to sign my contract, leaving me little time to review its contents. I met with a retired superintendent, who coached me through some technical issues, and then I met with the district's legal counsel. In retrospect, I signed a mediocre contract.

During my second superintendency, I hired an expert to negotiate a stellar contract for me. Take my advice, and seek out state advisory groups who offer contract help, or hire a professional educational negotiator to guide you through this process.

In California, for example, our administrative association, called ACSA, supports a professional standards department, which offers a free service to all members, as a part of their dues. Check out your state's associations for similar services.

Signed, Sealed, and Delivered—Right?

Don't be so quick to pack up your desk and throw a farewell party, just yet. Horror stories abound over those resigning from their districts early, only to find out that the hiring district reversed their decision. Sometimes the new district loses funding for the position and changes direction mid-stream. Sometimes new information becomes available; information not mentioned in the interview or disclosed on the paperwork, and the district has a change of heart. These are exceptions, of course, but be mindful and cautious when resigning.

There are two distinct acts that occur, relative to each position: (1) new hires are board approved by the district, and the candidate signs either a contract or an intent to hire form; and (2) employees hired in a new district must officially resign, *in writing*, from their former district or position.

Do not resign, until you are board approved by your new district. Do not let anyone force you to resign, before the new job is board approved. Don't let anyone pressure you into resigning, so they can fill your former position. Districts can screen and anticipate hiring a replacement, based on your tentative hire, alone. They do not need a resignation.

Don't play Russian Roulette with your career. Be strategic and steadfast in your conviction. Ninety-nine percent of the time, everything works out well, but it's no secret that these situations can cause some restless nights.

The Transition Plan

For most applicants, securing a new promotion is thrilling. After the planning, preparation, researching, strategizing and sleepless nights—one wants to celebrate, right? Not always.

If you've had a good run in your current district, people may be angry that you chose to leave them. Those who didn't care for you all along will now feel free to unleash pent up feelings, which may hurt. As a matter of proper protocol, write a letter to your employees, and share how much you liked working with them. Encourage them to stay the course with their goals, and ensure them you will stay connected and visit.

When I left districts, I bought small gifts for my secretary, principals, and close associates. They became my family away from home. It is difficult to leave, but moving on is a natural part of the promotional process. I have worked in six school districts over a span of many years and still have contact with colleagues in all six districts. Facebook and email are amazing ways for keeping in touch with former colleagues.

It also helps, when taking a new position, to have a plan in place to ease the transition. As a consultant, I offer a highly successful One Hundred Day Plan for superintendents. Activities during the first 100 days of any leadership transition are critically important. The purpose of following a 100 day plan is to ensure that, during this transition period, the organization will continue to focus on steady academic progress and management efficiency. Strategies included in a transition plan help to:

- Quickly gather information about the community and the organization.
- Foster an immediate relationship with the Board of Education and key stakeholders.
- Establish an early and strong community presence.
- Identify critical issues; correct weaknesses; build on strengths.
- Create a network of contacts and resources to assist the new administrator.
- Provide an entry plan to build upon the district's successful foundation of school improvement and progress.

I suggest, as a new administrator, you spend your first few weeks getting to know the people you will be working with. Whenever I moved to a new district, I offered the district a biography to use for public relations and press releases. I also requested that the district help me arrange a "meet and greet" to establish positive relationships and earn public trust, as soon as possible. As a new principal, I worked with the PTA and asked them to host a reception for me to meet the community. As a superintendent, the Board of Trustees sponsored an event to meet with key stakeholders. These events increased my personal knowledge of the district and community, its culture, tradition, history and expectations.

Warm up Exercises—Interview Prep

Competition for top leadership positions is increasing. To win against this stiff competition, you will need to be your absolute best. When the race is neck and neck, the prize goes to the person that brought their "game."

As you know, a marathon runner doesn't just wake up one morning, put on running shoes and head out to compete, without having prepared months in advance. The interview process is much like running a marathon. In order to excel and win the job, advanced preparation is required.

During the interview, the panel asks many questions designed to test your confidence, poise, and desirable personality traits. Sometimes questions will trick you into contradicting yourself, and others will probe your decision making and leadership ability. In your attempt to win the race, four major speed bumps have the potential to slow you along the way:

1. Not hearing the question correctly.
2. Answering a question that was not asked.
3. Providing unnecessary information or answering a question off the cuff, without thinking.
4. Attempting to dominate the interview.

You cannot prepare for every possible question asked. In working with executive mentoring clients, I have found it more effective for them to think about key themes to use throughout the interview. These themes represent key areas in educational leadership that are likely to surface in an interview.

What follows below are examples of selected key themes. I refer to these examples as "Scrimmage Notes," designed to help you prepare for an interview. Practice making up questions around these themes. It makes good sense to have an arsenal of ideas and concepts stored away and ready to use during the interview.

For example, every interview for educational leadership asks a question related to student achievement. The question will present itself in different forms, shapes, and sizes, and you must be prepared to answer it. I've seen many applicants' eyes glaze over, when a question related to student achievement is asked. Typically, candidates who are not prepared, approach this question in a scattergun fashion, hoping to hit something. As an interviewer, I'm always left feeling—does this person really know anything about what we do with students? Could this person put a plan in place to raise student achievement?

There are core areas one must internalize, in order to succeed in an educational administration interview. Once you master these content areas, you will be able to answer almost any question in the interview. You probably already know the answers, and they aren't trick questions. You just need to prepare properly for them in advance. Answering basic educational questions on the fly can be difficult, even for the most seasoned administrator. That's why those working in top positions of leadership, *practice, practice, practice,* to refine their interview skills.

For example, I've seen quality candidates fall down on simple questions related to teaching and learning. This question is an easy one: "Tell us what you want to see when you go into a teacher's classroom. Explain what you believe to be effective teaching." This question should be easy, right? You can't imagine what I've heard from unprepared applicants.

A highly respected high school principal, applying for an assistant superintendent of educational services, talked for nearly three minutes about his desire to observe student work displayed on classroom bulletin boards. As educators, we know student work is important, but there's a lot more to it than that. This candidate never mentioned any other components of good teaching. He never talked about student engagement, teaching to an objective, classroom management, assessment, or instructional delivery—just student work on the bulletin board. If this candidate wanted to be an assistant superintendent of educational services, he would need to answer an instructional question a lot better than he did.

Now that we're on the same page, let's focus our attention on the details of preparing for your next interview.

SCRIMMAGE NOTES

As an executive mentor, I like to use the word "scrimmage" as a metaphor to emphasize the most important aspect of the interview process—the practice. A scrimmage is an informal sports contest or practice match, engaged in for practice purposes, which does not count in the regular season record. [Wikipedia]. Scrimmages are not official, but athletes try to play them like the real thing. Scrimmages are advantageous, because athletes can work out plays in advance, and get a sense for how they will play in the real game.

I have created a group of interview (scrimmage) notes to use in the preparation phase of your job search. You must be able to speak intelligently, and cite examples relative to each area.

The contents of each area have the potential to surface in any question. Sometimes a question can cover two areas. For example: 1) How do you use assessment to (2) improve student learning? Use the following notes and samples to craft out your own answers to questions related to your skills and experience set.

Please remember once again, it is not effective to memorize answers to a hundred different interview questions. You do, however, need to be ready with tip-of-tongue stories and examples that substantiate your competencies, motivation, and ability to deliver results.

Keep in mind that your number one goal in an interview is to get the employer and panel members to connect with you, personally, so they can identify with you and begin to like you. Panel members constantly ask themselves throughout a candidate's interview, "Do we want to work with this person?" If you have content area knowledge internalized, you will be at ease in the interview, making it easier for the panel to connect with you.

I suggest you begin the process of preparing, by making a small notebook. Write each topic listed on a page, and then add your personal examples and relevant information. Then plan to review your notes just before the interview, in order to gain added confidence.

Greatest Strengths

You should know what your greatest strengths are. They should be related to your job skills. Don't try to think them up during the interview. Be able to discuss three of your major strengths, and be able to cite an example for each one. Think about how to weave each strength into questions during the interview. These are strengths you really believe in—ones you have consistently demonstrated over time.

Some strengths may include, planning, decision making, good communicator, knowledge of instruction, collaborator, team builder, etc. For example, you could respond to a question related to your greatest strengths in the following way:

With over twenty years of experience as a teacher and administrator, I offer three key strengths that are closely aligned to your needs for this position.

First, I am an excellent planner and know how to plan with the end goal in mind, working backwards to develop the steps necessary to bring in a project on time. I have provided leadership for the development of our district's strategic plan that included key stakeholders from the school district.

Second, I am an excellent team builder. I know how to build positive relationships, and bring people together for a common purpose. For example, I recently established a district team to address the dropout problem in our district. We created a program that will be implemented at each school to target potential dropouts, and provide intervention services.

Finally, I have a strong background in curriculum and instruction. I have worked on many projects to increase student achievement, such as the creation of Professional Learning Communities, in which all teachers meet to examine student work, and discuss strategies to improve their instructional delivery.

Outstanding Qualities or Words Colleagues Use to Describe You

Think of words to describe your personality. This question comes in all forms. It's good to have three or four desirable words (integrity, sense of humor, trustworthiness, people person) to describe your character and personality, and be able to give an illustration for each one:

My colleagues say I have a great sense of humor and am a very positive person. I always try to bring the best out of everyone. After all, we are in the people business and students are fun to be around. I try to find something constructive to say to everyone during their workday.

What do you know about the district? How will you impact their vision?

Your response should include both an understanding of the district and their students. Be informed. You must do some basic research. You don't need to go overboard, by researching every little detail, memorizing test scores, or listing programs to recite. You should be able to give a cursory overview of their district or school plan, and know key points.

Since every district/school wants to improve student achievement, be prepared to tell them how you plan to enhance that vision, by providing exemplary and challenging programs for students. You can address this question around three elements:

1. **Assess**: Assess what is already going well.
2. **Validate**: Acknowledge those efforts and accomplishments.
3. **Extend your leadership**: Finally, after a few weeks and/or months on the job, describe to them how you plan to extend your visionary leadership—integrity, relationship building, team building—to bring their district/school to a new level of excellence.

Improve Student Achievement

This question can be answered from many different angles. If applying for site level positions, answer as a *school* question, and if applying to district level positions, respond from the *total organizational perspective*. Stay focused on a few specific elements you can address in within five minutes.

A word of caution. This question has the potential to take an applicant off in many different directions. You need to focus on a few key areas, and stay in the driver's seat.

Address at least four or five main points, in order to answer this question effectively. Use these points as guidelines to focus your discussion on continued academic improvement. On the surface, this question sounds overwhelming, but actually it's an easy one. Just think about what you do every day in your job, and tell your story.

Also, describe how you have played a role in your current job or how you intend to work in your new role to improve student achievement, by addressing these core areas:

- Determine definition of academic achievement—grade level standards, language proficiency, student test scores, report card grades, good citizenship, attendance, graduation rate, etc.
- Set realistic goals and benchmarks.

- Provide researched based instructional delivery.
- Manage and use assessment.
- Implement intervention/acceleration programs.
- Build professional learning communities.
- Measure and hold people accountable.
- Validate accomplishments.

Building Trust

Since it is extremely important for a school district to hire a person they can trust, questions will be asked to determine if you are a trustworthy person. Your trustworthiness will be gauged in the interview, by how well you have demonstrated trusting behavior in your current district. This can be accomplished by backing up knowledge and belief statements with personal examples, such as:

I believe it's important for a leader to be visible, and as a school principal, I personally greet every student in the morning, as they come to school.

A panel also measures trust by an applicant's affability in the interview. As a result, it's essential that you try to "be yourself," and attempt to share a few personal examples, such as your dealings with a difficult employee or a challenge you are working through. It's also critical to share that you value transparency in all district communication (related to trust building).

Since the topic of trust may not surface directly in a question, remember to address trust issues on your own, throughout the interview. Share examples that demonstrate you are a person of your word, that you follow through with promises, that you believe in sharing information openly and honestly, and that you can be trusted.

Some specific examples to show you are trustworthy include:

- Building and communicating a transparent budget.
- Forming advisory groups to keep information open and honest.
- Following through on what you say you will do.
- Maintaining confidentially.

Leadership Style

You may be asked if you consider yourself a natural leader or a born follower. Don't get caught up trying to teach the panel the difference between a leader, manager, or follower, since a good leader usually demonstrates all three. Rather, be prepared to share your leadership style, and speak from your experience on this question. As a student of educational leadership, you will have read many leadership books and articles and will have identified your own personal style.

There is no right or wrong answer to this question, but some important styles panels respond to include: (1) visionary leadership; (2) collaborative leadership; and (3) servant leadership.

Perhaps you want to talk about how you are a visionary leader. If you choose that style, discuss how educators are charged with taking their schools/districts to new levels of excellence. In order to do that, a leader needs to have a vision of where they want to take them. Once a leader has a vision in place, they need to develop a plan to make their vision a practical reality. Since great leaders know they can't do it alone, they must build teams (talk about collaboration). Speak from experience, and share how you intend to take your followers to a new place. (This is a great place for a quote).

A Problem—and How You Dealt With It

Don't stress out over this question. You merely want to convey to the interviewer how you go about solving problems. Select a problem that doesn't involve dealing with difficult people, as it might appear you are criticizing others. Choose a few problems in advance, from the work situation that had a good ending.

This is a favorite question. Keep in mind that it's not so much the problem itself that's important—it's the approach you take to solving problems in general the panel wants to hear about. A question related to problem solving is designed to probe your professional and analytical skills. For example, "How did the problem arise, did you blame anyone, and what did you do to solve the problem?"

Begin to digest the problem with the panel, by using this simple formula:

1. **Problem identification**: Step back and think about the problem; identify the actual core of the problem.

2. **Underlying or related causes**: What caused the problem? Could it be a symptom of another problem? Are there any hidden factors to think about?

3. **Problem solution**: Make a list of possible solutions, and determine feasibility.

4. **Solution selection**: Weigh pros and cons of each solution, and determine the best solution.

5. **Implement solution**: How do you communicate your recommendation? What is your plan for implementation and process for including district stakeholders?

Here is a sample response:

When dealing with challenging situations in the workplace, I like to step back and gain some perspective on the situation. I like to generate ideas about how to solve the problem, which often involves collaborating with others and then prioritizing the options. If I need to gain approval from my supervisors before implementing, I present the options and recommendation to them in advance. Finally, I follow through and implement the solution. Let me give you an example....

Talk about your situation, using the problem solution formula above.

Traits and Skills of a Successful Administrator

Use this opportunity to show how well you've done your homework researching the duties for the position. State what you understand to be the key competencies needed for this leadership position, and show how your skills are a good match for this job. The panel may want to know how you envision success in your new role.

Some specific skills in which every administrator must demonstrate proficiency include:

- Communication
- Instructional leadership
- Organizational skills
- People skills
- Assessment
- Decision making
- Knowledge of curriculum, finance, school law
- Consensus builder

Rather than list them, select a few to share with the panel, and give an example of how you have demonstrated mastery over time.

Define how you measured your success. For example, you might say you believe that, in order to be an outstanding administrator, one needs to be an excellent communicator.

Share some examples of how you communicate—regular newsletters, advisory forums, and websites.

Provide an example of how you determine your success—surveying employees to learn if they feel communication is clear, ongoing and transparent.

> **INSIDER TIP**
> When sharing a success story use the "It's about them, not me," perspective.

The Effective Teacher

An interview panel will try to determine what you know about teaching and learning, by asking a series of probing questions. One of those questions will focus on the teacher, as a way to determine your depth of knowledge in this subject area. The teacher question can take a variety of forms:

- How would you evaluate a teacher?
- What do you look for when you go into a teacher's classroom?
- When you hire a teacher, what qualities will you look for in making your decision?

You should know three to four exemplary teaching elements, and be able to intertwine them into the teacher quality question.

An approach to this question might involve discussing core areas related to teaching and learning and describing specific details pertinent to each area. Four areas to begin that conversation could take the following form. When I hire a new teacher, I always look for four main qualities:

1. Knowledge of subject or content.
2. Ability to put this knowledge into a meaningful instructional lesson.
3. Classroom management skills.
4. Most important—does this teacher like and relate well to students?

Conflict Resolution

You may be asked to relate your experience with a recent conflict. Select a conflict that highlights your ability to negotiate, and use consensus. Think about a conflict you have managed in advance, that you are comfortable sharing. Be mindful that some conflicts have the potential to downplay a lack of skills or experience, so select a conflict that shows your involvement in a positive light.

The conflict you chose could involve an issue between the school and a parent, two teachers, or your dealings with a student. Ensure the conflict you select has a good ending and is not too controversial.

Some ideas to reflect upon when mediating a conflict include:

1. Separate people from the problem, by trying to identify the problem.
2. Put yourself in their shoes.
3. Deal with emotion first; substance second. Ask probing questions to lower the volume in the room and engender empathy.
4. Ask, "What would you like to see happen?"
5. Guide—don't decide.
6. Help all parties leave every interaction with grace and not regret.

Navigating Change Process

Change is inevitable in schools and, for that matter, in any job you apply for. Be prepared to explain a recent change you have dealt with and the plan you used to navigate the change process. Again, don't spend time in the interview pondering over what change to talk about. Rather, act like you're thinking over the question, and collect your thoughts concerning how you will approach the change question.

Here are a few steps to consider, when crafting out your response to the change question:

1. **Analysis**: What is the change, and why was it needed?
2. **Planning**: What kind of a plan was created to implement the change?
3. **Implementation**: Once you have developed a plan, what did you do to help people implement the change? Did you provide staff development and ongoing communication?
4. **Evaluation**: Every successful change is evaluated in terms of what went right or wrong and what needs to be refined.

Make sure you select an example of a change that turned out well. Yes—make it a successful change.

Making People Accountable

When you hear the word "accountability" connected with those you work with, a panel wants to know how you are going to get people to follow your leadership, without experiencing a "Mutiny on the Bounty" situation.

Listen carefully to how the question is worded. If you hear, "How will you provide accountability for our educational program?"—talk about instruction. If the panel asks how you will provide accountability for student discipline—talk about a school discipline or safety plan. But if they ask, "How will you hold people accountable, delegate authority, assign responsibly, and maintain account-ability?"—think of subordinates. Keep your answers simple, and listen for key words to guide your response in the right direction.

If you are asked, "How will you make people accountable?"— here are a few pointers:

- **Assign responsibility**: Ensure that your employees know their roles and responsibilities in the job. It's hard to help people improve or expect greatness from them, when they don't know what they are supposed to be doing.
- **Delegate**: Learn to delegate to others, and subtly share your power. You have to assume the people you hired can do the job.
- **Support**: Your job as a leader is to provide support, and let people know you are there to help them, when necessary. Disciplined employees can get the upper hand, when confronted with poor performance that was not documented. For example, "You never told me what to do or how to improve in this area, and you didn't give me any help."
- **Monitor**: Use "management by walking around" and regular conferences to assess if people are doing what you expect of them.

Remember to be on guard for this question. Just when you think you are on top of the interview, the "accountability question" rears its head. You are now prepared to discuss accountability issues for those you supervise.

Making Decisions

When asked a "decision making question," you can address it in two ways. First, state how you can make an immediate decision (the 911) and are able to direct people to carry out a quick decision. Secondly, talk about the real heart and soul of this question—how you make long term decisions, involving collaboration that affect people's lives.

Think about a few decisions you have made recently, and use them as examples. Prepare a few "rehearsed" decisions in advance, and be ready to talk about the decision making process you used:

1. Use a collaborative process, and consider all viewpoints to form a common thread.
2. Collect enough information to make an informed decision. Ultimately weigh what's good for students.
3. Evaluate the decision after implementation.

Communication

A high priority with interviewees is to determine exactly how well you communicate with staff, students, and parents. This question can be very broad and take many different forms, but a good starting point is to share that you communicate honestly, openly, and frequently.

You believe knowledge is power. I suggest you surround the communication topic with examples of how well you have communicated with others in your current position. There are two overarching communication goals that can take your answer in a positive direction:

1. Improving one-way communication for all stakeholders to obtain information, such as newsletters, email, telephone messages, forums, etc.
2. Creating settings to enhance two-way communication, such as advisory councils, meetings, symposiums.

The Budget

Depending upon what position you intend to fill, this question can be answered in many different ways. At the assistant principal level, a panel will ask about your experience with school budgets. It is important for an aspiring administrator to gain credible experience with school budgets through his/her mentor.

Perhaps you have worked with a department budget and allocated resources to your colleagues. Be prepared to back up this question with demonstrated experiences in the field, to show your budget knowledge.

If you have no budget experience, inform the panel that: (1) you are excited to learn about the inner workings of a school budget; (2) are a fast learner; and (3) will do what it takes to be a contributor to a successful school budget.

On the other hand, if you are applying for a school principal position, you will be expected to know how to develop a school budget that is aligned with your school's goals. Talk about your work on the school plan and your comfort level with categorical, formula dollars, and discretionary funding.

A question at the district level will probe to learn about your budgetary expertise, as well as your ability to mitigate a budget crisis. At the superintendent level, you will be asked to discuss your experience with budget development.

If asked how you will address the declining resources facing our nation's schools, consider talking about working with your team to create a budget stabilization plan. A stabilization plan has four facets and can apply to both site and district levels:

1. **Reductions**: Discuss how you will make budget reductions in both the current and upcoming budgets. Mention that you will not call reductions "cuts," since this term leaves people thinking entire programs may be slashed (their jobs). As part of the reduction process, share that you will develop and communicate a restoration plan for those areas eliminated, if and when funding returns.

2. **Efficiencies**: Talk about how you intend to review current services to determine what can be consolidated, in order to become more efficient (i.e. bus routes, overlap of services). An example might include a review of special education services that can be replicated in-house, rather than contracting out.

3. **Revenue enhancement**: Suggest ideas that will bring additional money to schools or the district, such as creating foundations, charging for services, implementing fund raisers, or participating in more grant writing.

4. **Budget Flexibility**: Finally, share that, as part of a stabilization plan, you intend to use every penny possible for intended services. For example, many school districts are unaware that grant and categorical funds can be used for special education.

Assessment

Assessment and use of data is a big topic of concern in education. Educators have come a long way over the past decade, concerning their philosophy and use of data to drive instructional issues. If the assessment question is asked, prepare to discuss how you have used assessment data in your current role to set goals, improve instruction, or make decisions. Also, be prepared to share how you intend to use assessment in your new role.

To demonstrate your understanding of assessment, you may want to cover some of the following issues:

1. The purpose of data is to "improve" not to "prove."
2. Data must be valid and reliable.
3. Data must be responsibly collected and managed.
4. Teachers should use data in Professional Learning Communities (PLCs).
5. Data should guide instructional choices—lesson delivery, curriculum purchases, program implementation.

English Language Learners

If you apply to a district with a large English language learner population, you can expect a question on how you will improve their academic and language skills. This question will be difficult to navigate, if you haven't considered a response in advance. The question can also cause concern in the interview, if you lack experience working with English language learners. You must approach the question in a way that shows you have core knowledge about English language students and be able to share strategies for how you would deliver an instructional program to meet the needs of English language learners.[7]

[7]Students may be referred to as English language learners, Second language learners, or English Language Development students. There are many other terms used nationwide, but essentially the student in question lacks English as their primary language.

Here is a sample response for a question related to English language learners:

> *In my current district I have worked to improve achievement for our English language learners, by providing them equal access to all of our educational programs. I ensure that our assessment system is accurate and dependable, so that it places students in appropriate classes to meet their needs. Once placed in classes, these students need to have access to qualified teachers, who know how to provide instructional support to second language learners.*
>
> *As an instructional leader, I ensure that our teachers have access to researched based instructional materials and are well trained in second language teaching strategies. English language learners can get trapped in the system, as a result of poor assessment techniques or rigid master scheduling practices.*

I like to share a metaphor, to explain my philosophy for providing an outstanding educational program to second language learners in the public school system. As educators, we want all of our students on the right path—a *freeway*, so to speak—to become career, college ready students.

Second language learners have difficulty getting access to the "freeway." They often get placed on a permanent "country road" that runs alongside the freeway, with little or no access to the freeway.

We as educators must create on-ramps or program strategies that give these students access to the freeway. We must provide English language support but must also teach them what the majority of students are learning.

There is no "one size fits all" program for these students; rather it's more about where these kids belong, getting them clear access to on-ramps that lead to the freeway—good teachers, workable master schedules, materials, and meaningful assessments.

Special Education—Gifted and Talented

The chance of a special education or GATE question being asked often depends upon the composition of the district and, in some cases, an interest of a specific panel member (special education teacher or GATE parent). So you need to be prepared. Some general themes to consider:

Special education and gifted and talented education (GATE) are *not places*. Rather, these designations refer to the *delivery of services* to support students with special needs. There is an abundance of research to address these areas, so it is important to have an opening statement, regarding where to take your answer.

Don't resort to citing research. Articulate that you believe an administrator must work with key stakeholders, to provide support to special students. Give examples of your experience working with these student groups (programs, supervision, own child), and share how you intend to provide services to these student populations in your new job.

Work with Unions

It will be important to talk about your harmonious relationships with both classified and teacher unions, even if some of your experiences have been contentious. In the interview, discuss how much you value their work, and give positive examples of how you have collaborated with unions in your current role or in past experiences. For example, try to mention any participation in interest based bargaining or trust building sessions. Have you served on any advisory roles or, as a teacher, were you part of the union rep council?

Early in my career, I created a mnemonic device called the "T-Square for Collaboration"[8] that I shared with union leadership, as a school administrator. Each word began with a "T" and focused on key areas to help us remember how to maintain positive working relationships between bargaining units and administration.

This device may help you focus on areas to discuss, when asked a union question in an interview:

1. **Trust**: Develop trust by telling the truth and following through with promises.

2. **Transparency**: Share all information regarding budget, policies, new programs, etc. in an honest and open fashion.

3. **Teamwork**: Work with employee organizations, arm-in-arm, to solve problems that affect the school, union members, and most of all our students.

4. **Training**: Provide and attend trainings, (i.e. Speed of Trust, IBB) to enable positive relationship building and problem solving.

Diversity

When diversity questions are raised in an interview, candidates often have a tendency to concentrate mainly on the area of race. It is important to remember that diversity comes in all forms, and a school district wants to know how you are going to deal with all the various diversity issues and what you are doing in your current role to exercise leadership in this area.

Some types of diversity areas to mention include language, gender, religion, poverty, health concerns, parenting issues, etc. Some ways to answer a question on diversity include:

• Remember to state your overriding philosophy that you respect the cultural and individual differences of all people.

[8]T-Square for Collaboration ©Ryder and Associates

- As a leader, you will share your diversity philosophy with all stakeholder groups.
- You will work with district administrators and support staff to continually review and modify policies and programs that reflect issues of growing diversity.
- During the interview, give specific examples of how you have addressed diversity in your prior roles—recruiting teachers and staff, equal access to materials and core curriculum, parent involvement, providing student programs.

Dropout Prevention

Many school districts across the nation are experiencing a high student dropout rate. Districts are forming task forces to address this issue and are implementing some very effective anti-dropout programs.

Before interviewing, review any dropout programs the district has in place, and know the district's dropout rate. Be prepared to discuss their efforts to reduce the dropout rate, and include how you will complement their programs. If possible, detail any work you have done to address the dropout issue in your current role.

If asked how you would confront the dropout crisis, you can defer to key elements of successful dropout prevention programs.

- Identify potential dropouts—usually occurs in 7th and 9th grades.
- Dropout students have similar characteristics: (1) the majority of dropouts have average or above ability; (2) high absenteeism; (3) poor discipline records; (4) failing grades; (5) limited school engagement; (6) no participation in clubs or athletics.
- Once identified, student programs are developed around mentoring, tutoring, and intervention. All teachers are aware of the names of potential drop outs and are held accountable for providing additional support in their classrooms for these students.

- Community services and health support systems are engaged to work with the schools.

Positive Climate

We all want to work in a positive environment, and employers want to know how you intend to maintain or create a positive environment—especially if that's not their district's current situation.

Approach a question related to this topic, by sharing some strategies used throughout your career that have contributed to positive working climates:

1. **Clear Vision**: Vision of maintaining high standards for everyone and the belief that every child can learn. The vision is shared with everyone.

2. **Core Values**: Instill values of respect, caring, trustworthiness, and conflict resolution into the work environment.

3. **Honest and Open Communication**: Ensure that communication is two-way and that problems are shared.

4. **Team**: Hold everyone accountable, and implement team building activities to build team spirit.

Greatest Accomplishment

When you talk about your greatest accomplishment, it should be your biggest, most salient initiative. The interview panel is looking for the following:

- Your drive and energy.
- The most important idea or project you have personally set into motion.
- What you deem as significant.

Keep your greatest accomplishment current and related to the field of education—unless you have just saved someone's life, played pro football, been awarded an Oscar, or done something that shows you are extra-ordinarily exceptional, outside the field of education!

I experienced an interview session once, in which the candidate spent ten minutes discussing her greatest accomplishment, in stunning detail. The accomplishment was undeniably great, but it failed on all accounts, in that it occurred ten year earlier. After she left, the superintendent said, "Can you believe it? This woman's greatest accomplishment was over ten years ago! I want to hire someone whose greatest accomplishment occurred recently—not ten years ago." Another candidate indicated his greatest accomplishment was marrying his wife. It was amusing at the time, but not really what the panel was looking for.

Think about something you have done to help a student or a program, that made a difference for the school. Talk about something that required a lot of work, creativity, involved a plan, and necessitated collaboration. Have your latest and greatest accomplishment memorized. Remember—if you are not asked about your greatest accomplishment, try to work it into an answer for another question, if possible.

Five Years From Now

Districts want to hire someone who will stay forever, but in reality, we all know that probably won't happen. In addition, if you are sporting some gray hair, panels will attempt to open a dialog concerning your retirement plans. I recommend a response, something like this:

Hopefully, I'll be working here, in this position. I envision myself working in a position of leadership, at least five to ten more years.

Note: Never discuss your retirement plans in an interview.

Technology

It's a rare interview that won't ask about your level of expertise with technology. Recognize that a district doesn't actually want to know about your personal "tech" proficiency (although that helps), but they want to learn about your vision for implementing technology in their district and how you have demonstrated attaining that goal in your past experiences.

Notice that many questions not only want you to think forward with your answers, but also to show proof that you have followed through and have actual experience managing technology plans. In other words, talk means nothing to a panel, unless you can back it up with past experience.

Be prepared to discuss your technology vision, a plan for making that a reality in their school district, and talk about your demonstrated experience:

- **Vision**: Technology is a tool to engage students, help them learn, and prepare them to work in our global society.

- **Practical Reality**: Develop a technology plan that includes updated infrastructure, hardware, and staff development. Ensure that all purchases are directly related to increased student achievement. Remember that integrating technology is more about changing attitude and spirit and less about skill.

- **Sample Experience**: In my current district, I implemented Promethium Boards in every classroom, as a way to engage students in the curriculum, and as a result, student test scores soared.

What Do You Have Left to Learn?
or Greatest Weakness

This question is asked a lot and, in my opinion, is ineffective. Most applicants will have practiced this answer in advance and won't need help from this book. They manage a standard answer for turning a weakness into strength:

I enjoy my work and always give 100% on every project. When people don't pull their weight, I get a bit unnerved. I am aware of my weakness in this area, and I try to be more understanding with people's family schedules, that sort of thing, and give back a positive attitude.

That answer is okay but gets a smile from most of us. This particular "weakness" is probably written in a lot of self-help books, because panel members hear it quite often.

I'd rather hear something like:

I have difficulty learning software, but I do consider myself a lifelong learner. Right now, I am trying to learn how to manage the software program "Publisher" to create my own newsletters. It's not an easy program, for sure—but I won't be happy, until I create my first publication. I find that keeping up with new technology programs can be a daunting challenge, but once I learn a new program, I'm on my way to the next one.

Pick an area in which you are honestly trying to improve. When you give a concrete example of a weakness, and then detail how you intend to address this weakness, you gain a lot of credibility. Some panels have created a variation on this question and now ask:

Out of the four areas needed for this position: (1) expertise in curriculum and instruction; (2) finance; (3) personnel; or (4) board relationships—what area do you feel the strongest in, and what area the weakest?

If you run across this question, be aware that it has a dual purpose. Not only are they assessing strengths and weaknesses, but they are looking for any red flags you might disclose, while answering the question. Keep it simple, and talk about wanting to enhance all four areas.

Last Book Read

A panel may ask what book you last read. This will be your opportunity to show the panel that you keep up with professional development in the field. This is definitely not the place to to discuss your favorite book on job searches, mysteries, or love stories.

If you make reference to a book, just make sure you have read it, in case there are any follow-up questions about the book. I recall an applicant referring to his latest book read, *Overcoming the Five Dysfunctions of a Team,* when answering a question about team building. It was unfortunate he hadn't read the book. Two principals on the panel loved the book and wanted to engage in some small talk. The applicant couldn't recall *one* of the five dysfunctions. The silence in the room was deadly.

Hobbies, Fun, Relaxation, etc.

I always asked applicants applying for leadership positions what they do outside of work to relax, have fun, and share time with friends and family.

Note: Be careful not to share a controversial activity or risky behaviors:

- Campaigning for a political party—potential to offend panel members belonging to the other political parties.
- Drinking parties—offends everyone.
- Race car driving or sky diving—possibly won't show up for work on Monday.

Student Safety

Preparing an answer for this topic depends upon the level of the position you are applying to. A question for an assistant principal will deal with individual student discipline issues, while one for a superintendent will probably address comprehensive district safety plans. Create an outline to approach this question appropriate to the position.

Safety plans will provide the infrastructure, such as student rules of conduct, board policies, and organization of daily procedures. Two key areas to address when discussing student safety include:

1. **Prevention**: Proactive programs you have worked with or created to make schools safe and secure—bullying curriculum, Character Counts, parent and community advisory boards.

2. **Intervention**: What you have done to assist those needing help—drug counseling or testing, mentoring programs, intervention, community service.

Components of an Outstanding School District

When asked to talk about an exemplary school district or requested by a panel to describe the components of an outstanding school, there is a simple way to organize your thinking in advance to approach this topic.

As an assistant superintendent, I developed a prompt to help people understand the various components of an educational program. I call the structure a COST Analysis.[9]

Simply put, each letter in the word COST signifies an area of discussion that summarizes key facets of an educational program. Use this device as a way to cover main areas, to describe an educational delivery program for a school or an entire school district.

[9]COST Analysis ©Ryder and Associates

COST Analysis©

Focus Areas	Sample Discussion Points for Each Area
Curriculum and Instruction	**Standards**: Are standards guaranteed for every grade level; do pacing guides exist; can the curriculum be delivered in one school year? **Curriculum**: Are researched based instructional materials provided and used? **Instruction:** Do teachers use researched based instructional practices in their classroom? **Assessment**: Are assessment strategies timely, meaningful, and are results used to drive instructional decisions?
Organizational Structure	**Personnel**: Are the best employees hired? Does an effective evaluation system exist? **Finance and Resources**: Are district resources used effectively to improve teaching and learning? Is the budget balanced and developed to support student programs? **Technology**: Does technology directly support student learning and district efficiency? **Discipline and Safety Plans**: Do these plans allow for student and employee safety? **Communication Plans**: Does the organization have a solid plan to deliver ongoing, relevant information, in a timely manner?
Support	**Student Support**: Are special populations identified and programs developed to assist at risk, GATE, high achieving, or special education? **Staff Support**: Is staff development ongoing and provided for continuous learning? **Teacher Support**: Are teachers meeting in professional learning communities to assess student data and improve their instructional delivery? **Parent Support**: Are protocols in place to engage parents and help them be partners in their child's success? **Leadership Support**: Is leadership development encouraged at all levels, and do protocols exist that encourage new leadership within the district?

T̲eam

Vision: Has leadership staff developed a vision and plan for where the district is headed?
Team: Does the district have a team building attitude and a focus in which everyone is held accountable for student achievement?
Inclusion: Are parents and community members encouraged to be part of the "team?"

"Quotes"

I never used quotes in an interview, because they are not my style —but I have seen many applicants use quotes quite eloquently. Here's how it works with quotes:

- Make sure you are comfortable with the quote and its application, and only use one quote per interview.
- Offer two quotes, and you may be perceived as a "show off."
- Offer three quotes—and the panel might even think you've applied for the wrong job.

Heartfelt Story

Try to include at least one story in your interview. Tell a story that is appropriate, but only if it fits nicely into a specific question or can be used as part of your exit strategy. Don't tell a story, however, just for the sake of telling a story.

When interviewing for a superintendent position, I shared a story about my passion for working with students. Here's my story, with subtle, non-stated messages highlighted:

*For the past ten years, I've been running a mile every day before work. [**I'm loyal—ten years is a long time.**] I like to run to keep my weight stable, get exercise, and improve my overall mental state and well-being. [**I'm a healthy and energetic person.**]*

One day I ran a little later than usual. About midway through the run, I saw a school bus picking up a large group of kindergartners. I paused to look at these little ones and suddenly was overcome with an intense passion for my profession. I thought how lucky I was to have a job, in which I *could devote my life to children. **[I love students and my profession.]** Even though I observe and talk to students every day at work, **[I spend time at schools.]***

This day was different—the yellow bus, the large cluster of small children all walking in a row, getting on their school bus that would take them to school. It was a special moment; one that made me clearly aware of how important my work is and that I was making a difference in the lives of children and their future.

***[I believe my job is more than just a job.]** Maybe the endorphins from running caused this sensation, but it doesn't matter. Every day I reflect on how lucky I am to work in the field as an educational leader. **[I am a leader.]** Watching these babies, as they climbed onto the bus, made me recognize how important my work is and how lucky I am to be an educator. I love what I do and just wanted to share these feelings in this interview.*

This story had a strong impact on the board of trustees sitting on the interview panel, and they later hired me as their superintendent. They shared that my story was one of the defining reasons why they selected me to be their superintendent. When they were interviewed by the media, on my appointment to superintendent, the board president quoted my phrase from the interview: "Babies on the bus."

The story I shared with the board during this interview came from my heart and was true for me. Now, start to think about your own story—make it real, and share it.

Why Hire You?

Whenever I sat on an interview panel, I always asked every applicant the following questions:

I have a lot of quality candidates that have interviewed for this position. Why should we hire you?

In my experience, there is no right or wrong answer to this question. The candidate's answer, however, always gave me a good perspective into their motivation and whether I wanted to have this candidate join our team.

Your answer should be concise and to the point. Highlight areas from your background that relate to the job. Finish by reemphasizing your key strengths and talents—you've got them memorized, right? Say something, from your heart again, about your desire to be a valuable member of their high functioning team, or your intention to work tirelessly to make a difference for students.

You know why you want the job, why they should hire you—now tell them. And when you do, make eye contact with each person sitting around the table. Make it clear that you want the position!

Parting Shots

It's now time to review the focus areas in this chapter, and outline them to suit your own needs. Create your own interview template to study, and include a copy in your notebook. Use these notes to study and review, just before interviewing, to give you added confidence.

In summary, here are some important Interview "Do's" and "Don'ts."

Interview "Do's"

✅ Pre-visualize yourself in a successful interview.

✅ Know what's in your resume, and be prepared to discuss your qualifications for the job.

✅ Research and learn as much as possible about the position and the school district.

✅ Be ready to describe your strengths and weaknesses.

✅ Practice opening and closing statements.

✅ Practice interviewing with a friend or relative.

✅ Dress professionally in clothing resembling that of a school administrator.

✅ Review the location of the interview.

✓ As an extra measure, practice getting to the interview location in your car.

✓ Be on time.

✓ Turn off all electronic devices.

✓ Bring extra copies of your resume and list of references.

✓ Be courteous and respectful with everyone you meet.

✓ Make eye contact, and use a firm handshake.

✓ Show enthusiasm.

✓ Ask questions or seek clarification, if you aren't certain about a particular question.

✓ If you promise to follow up on something—do it.

✓ Accentuate the positive.

✓ Select and articulate relevant information for your responses. How can your skills and experience benefit the school district?

✓ Cite examples of past experiences and events to support your responses. Share your achievements and accomplishments, when appropriate.

✓ Be clear and concise. Keep each answer under three minutes.

✓ Remember to talk about students.

✓ Be confident, enthusiastic and honest.

✓ Smile!

Interview "Don'ts"

✗ Avoid slang.

✗ Avoid slouching.

✗ Avoid casual speech, such as leaving off word endings—workin' or improvin'—and don't use words like "betcha," "alrighty," or "kiddoes."

✗ Don't refer to a female superintendent as "Ma'am."

✗ Do not use the word "gal" to refer to females.

✗ Do not smoke just prior to the interview or chew gum during an interview.

✗ Don't ask about salary, sick days, or health insurance.

✗ Don't ask who your competition is.

✗ Don't say "my" principals, "my" teachers or "my" board.

❌Avoid saying "I" as much as possible. "We" and "our" are better terms.

❌Don't put the panel on the spot with hard to answer questions.

❌Keep your clothing accessories to a minimum.

❌If you must wear perfume, spray lightly. Some perfumes annoy people with allergies.

❌Avoid portfolios.

❌Don't be late.

Section V:

PERSEVERING - CROSSING THE FINISH LINE

Your goal is to secure a new position of leadership. We have covered *planning, packaging,* and *preparing*—and now a review of *perseverance* is in order. Perseverance is a quality you must have, if you want to turn your dream into a reality. I have included a final chapter on perseverance to help you "stay the course."

The following quote by Calvin Coolidge sums it up nicely:

Nothing in this world can take the place of persistence. Talent will not; nothing is more common than unsuccessful people with talent. Genius will not; unrewarded genius is almost a proverb. Education will not; the world is full of educated derelicts. Persistence and determination alone are omnipotent. The slogan, "press on" has solved and always will solve the problems of the human race.

Are you ready for some real inspiration? I love stories about people who reached success, despite the obstacles they faced. Here is a personal example of perseverance. I sent my manuscript to publishers, *The SeXX Factor: Breaking the Unwritten Codes that Sabotage Personal and Professional Lives* and received over forty rejection letters, before an editor finally took note and published my book.

Jack Canfield, author of *Chicken Soup for the Soul,* has shared his story of rejection with readers. His first manuscript was rejected by 123 different publishers! What we both have in common is *perseverance.*

Champions

Do you have a personal hero you think about, when the going gets tough? Let me share some of my inspirational champions:

Bill Gates: This genius dropped out of Harvard and failed in his first business attempt. We all know him as the man who created the global empire that is Microsoft.

Walt Disney: Walt had a bit of a rough start. He was fired by a newspaper editor, who thought he lacked imagination. He had several business failures that ended with bankruptcy. Of course, we all know he was a genius and one of the most successful Americans of all time.

Albert Einstein: Al didn't speak until he was four, and teachers worried he was mentally handicapped, when he couldn't read at age seven. He was also very anti-social and was eventually expelled from school. Most people think his ideas, however, turned out to be quite useful in the end.

Oprah Winfrey: Oprah was fired from her job as a television reporter, because she was "unfit for television." She also faced a hard road, enduring an abusive childhood. We all know her now as one of the wealthiest women in the world.

Jerry Seinfeld: The first time Jerry performed on stage at a comedy club, he was booed off the stage. Rumor has it that he encountered a huge case of stage fright. He had confidence in himself and returned the next night to rave reviews and laughter.

Lucille Ball: Before starring in the I Love Lucy show, Lucy was regarded as a "B" actress and told by her drama teachers to try another profession.

Elvis Presley: "You Ain't Nothin' but a Hound Dog" singer, was told after being fired by the manager of the Grand Ole Opry, "You aint' going nowhere son, you ought to go back to driving a truck."

Jack London: This well-known American author wasn't always such a success. His first story received six hundred rejection slips, before finally being accepted.

Harrison Ford: In his first film, Harrison was panned by movie execs and told that he simply didn't have what it takes to be a star.

[10]**Bud Bilanich. "Fifty Famous People who failed at their First Attempt at Career Success." 2012. <http://www.budbilanich.com/career-success-coach/50-famous-people-who-failed-at-their-first-attempt-at-career-success>**

Real People

Before writing this book, I contacted several colleagues and asked them if they would share some genuine moments about preserving against the odds, and offer advice to our colleagues about applying for jobs and interviewing. Most every person I asked to contribute was happy to help!

A point I tried to make earlier in this book was that, if you ask someone in the field to serve as your mentor, they probably won't turn you down. We are all involved in teaching and learning. We know that taking on a new career challenge can be difficult, and we have all experienced some form of defeat in our professions, at one time or another. The journey is not always easy, and as a result, we have learned from our mistakes and experiences.

Real Inspiration

As a superintendent, I hired a twenty-six year old woman to serve as the principal at one of our top performing elementary schools. She interviewed with two different panels. The first panel consisted of district administrators, and after the interview, they rated her as a top finalist. The second panel comprised of teachers, parents, and classified support staff liked her but thought she was too young to lead a school, and then rated her in the bottom half of the candidates. She managed to qualify as a top finalist, along with two other candidates, and later interviewed with the full executive cabinet and two board members.

During her interview, I was impressed with the knowledge, confidence, and poise she exhibited. Her teaching and curriculum expertise was superb. She shared a detailed vision for how she would take the school to a new level of excellence. As the superintendent, I knew I wanted to hire her to lead the school. I was equally excited that the other panel members also shared my perceptions and rated her number one.

While she was very young and lacked the years (in the field) often required for this top leadership position, I knew she had the personal qualities, leadership skills, and internal desire to be an outstanding leader. I hired her and was subsequently pleased with the choice.

As I watched her leadership development over the next two years, I was proud that she was leading one of our schools. She was the type of collaborative and visionary leader, who makes us all look good as educators. She is married, raises a young child, manages a high profile career, involves herself in the community, and competes regularly in athletic events, such as running marathons and triathlons.

On the day she interviewed, I remember her having a determined look in her eye and a noticeable high confidence level. I knew that she was on top of her game. She later shared that she views interviewing much like running a marathon.

I asked Sumer if she would share her thoughts about perseverance, when running a marathon. I sensed this young woman has a keen awareness of how the game is played and how to become a winner:

...There is a point in every race, when you consider, if only for a moment, slowing down or stopping. Countless hours of physical preparation only takes you so far. In that moment, you dig deep, and it's the mental game that takes over. You have to be prepared to push through pain, in order to reach new limits. As I near that mental wall, I repeat, "This is where champions are made," and keep pushing. You have to be willing to take risks—give it everything you have, for the remaining time or distance. You don't want to get to the end, and feel like you could have given it more, during the race.

Sumer Jackson
Director of Instruction

Coaches' Quarters

Below are some suggestions to help you sustain your motivation and desire to actualize your career goals. These are successful educators, who I admire and respect. They are the leaders of our future, and I value their opinions and the work they do for students. Listen to what they have to say!

Going through the entire promotion process is very difficult. You will apply, prepare, and interview for many more jobs than you will ever get. I have come in second place more times than I am willing to admit. There are powers at play throughout this process that you may never know or understand. There are internal applicants, friends, and contacts that may get a job over you, because of "fit" or favoritism. There are some districts and school boards who treat applicants in an unprofessional way.

You have to be ready and able to deal with rejection and a lack of professionalism.

> Getting a job can be more difficult than keeping or doing a job.

Getting a job is more difficult than keeping or doing a job. At the end of the day, the business of school is about relationships.

Remember that you need to be playing chess, while everyone else is playing checkers. Be strategic and stay the course!

Jeremy B. Nichols
Director of School Services

> Real leaders are relentless.

Real leaders are relentless. Being relentless means more than just not giving up. It means pushing through all comfort, convenience, challenge, and controversy. And in the face of your weakest moment, you'll perform like a Rock star!

Dr. Dale Marsden
Superintendent

I believe there are vital things one must do, in order to move ahead in their educational career. Finding a mentor is key. I have been very fortunate in my career to have outstanding people assist me in learning how to become an educational leader.

I encourage you to seek their guidance in how to perform your current role and what skills are needed to take the next step. Honest conversations about areas in which you need to improve should be seen as a positive thing.

Take advantage of any and all opportunities to increase your knowledge and skills in education. Professional administrative academies are a great way to learn about various roles in education. Get involved with organizations such as ACSA, CUE, and the regional League of Middle and High Schools. The networking *opportunities are valuable, providing you with resources for your current position, as well as future career opportunities.*

I would encourage you to participate on any district committee you can; negotiations, technology, strategic planning, etc. They will provide you with a greater understanding of the big picture, and demonstrate your desire to increase your leadership role. Finally, keep faith in yourself. Most applicants receive more "Thanks for your interest," than job offers.

> I encourage you to participate on district committees to learn the big picture.

The Navy SEALs teach that one should not dwell on the negative, and apply a positive spin to whatever you are doing. Attitude is everything, and can become a self-fulfilling prophecy. Positive energy and confidence attracts confidence from others.

Chad Wood
Director of Personnel

I've always compared job seeking to that of searching for a spouse; there are many out there, but you only need to find the one that fits best. The good thing about administrative jobs is that you will at some point outgrow the one you are currently in, and you will get to search for your next opportunity.

> I've always compared job seeking to that of searching for a spouse; there are many out there, but you only need to find the one that fits best.

In administrative job searching, you will need to perform a great deal of research about the school and district. Even if you do not get the job, you will undoubtedly learn something that you can use in your current position. Hang in there, there is a job just for you!

Brett Wolfe
High School Principal

Planning and packaging my paperwork and very intense interview preparation for every position I was looking at was the extra effort that got me noticed, as well as not taking "no" for an answer. When rejection hits, and it will, you must look at the rejection as a lesson,

155

and learn from every person you come into contact with, when trying move up the ladder.

Your entire application packet is your golden opportunity to let employers know why you are the best candidate for the position. I cannot tell you how many times I went over my résumé, line by line, and word for word, to make sure everything was in order.

> Your entire application packet is your golden opportunity to let employers know why you are the best candidate for the position.

Also, I would tailor my résumé and cover letter for each different position I was applying for. This showed that I took the time needed to recognize what each district was looking for and what I could offer. The application packet is not about what an employer can do for you, but what you can offer the employer.

Lastly, you must be well prepared for the interview. I researched every internet article, read every board agenda packet for the past year and looked at parent reviews for each district I was interested in. I made sure I knew the good, bad and ugly on each district. I also wanted to make sure it was a good fit for me.

One should not just blanket every job offering that is available with an application. I waited four years for the opportunity of a position that I felt would be a good fit for me, and that is where I am the Chief Business Officer today.

Michael Krause
Chief Business Official

Never underestimate the importance of researching the district and position for which you are applying.

> The interview is an opportunity for the district to decide if they want you, and also an opportunity for you to decide if you want to be there.

Some sage advice I received early on in my career goes something like this:

"The interview is an opportunity, not only for the district to decide if they want you, but also an opportunity for you to decide if you want to be there."

To this, I add—find out everything you can beforehand, to see if there is a potential fit for you. Read their board minutes, or even attend a board meeting. You can get a strong sense of the district's administration and board styles, which set the tone for the district's culture. Look up their performance statistics, research their finances and demographics. You don't need an overabundance of details, just some basic facts that you can include in the answers you will prepare for sample questions.

You will likely be asked what you know about the district or why you are applying there. You should have a thoughtful answer that demonstrates you know about the district, some of their strengths and challenges. Before you apply, you should discover if you have some ideas, skills or accomplishments that are congruent with their goals.

There are different approaches you can take to uncover this information. Call other administrators in the district to ask about the culture of the district, their goals, and any unique challenges that the district is facing. Be careful, many districts discourage applicants from talking to board members and administrators, sometimes to the point of dismissing an applicant because of this. Always begin the conversation with asking if there is any conflict in speaking to them about the position.

Ask, in the context of researching, to see if the role is one that suits your skills, and thank them for anything they are able to share with you. Be willing to pass on an interview, if the information you discover is a mismatch for your talents, work-style, or values.

Jeff Hinshaw
Chief Business Official

It's easy to get disappointed and lose confidence, when you are passed over for a job you really want. All too often, good candidates will stop applying, rather than risk rejection.

> My advice is to think of any selection procedure as a horse race.

My advice is to think of any selection procedure as a horse race. On any given day, one horse is going to be a nose faster than all the others, and it's not always the same horse. It depends on many factors in that particular race. Losing by a nose doesn't make you any the less a thoroughbred! Stay in the race, and continue to hone the skills that will help you to be a nose faster. The next race may see you in the winner's circle!

Dr. Patricia Clark White
Retired Superintendent

I recall a recent experience, wherein I'd made it through the paper screening and had completed a full battery of interviews and follow-up questions to become a School Transformation Coach, with a state department of education. I wanted this position, so that I could make a difference, by partnering with under-performing schools to transform the educational outcomes of students. I was especially interested in the position, because it complimented my work as Superintendent-in-Residence with the National Center for Urban School Transformation.

Perseverance, at times, is easier said than done. I'd done everything I was supposed to do, and there I was, waiting and wondering and waiting and wondering. I figured that the holdup was in processing my "paperwork."

I vividly reflected on my tenure months before, as an area superintendent, and the behind the scenes workings of the district's Human Resources division. I knew what it was like, when I processed things to hire principals for my cohort. Clearly, I knew that it would be equally—if not more—challenging to process my paperwork through a state department of education.

I didn't want to be a pest; however, I knew that maintaining communication was essential. I wrote the contact person for the position and learned that the team was impressed with my career experiences and my interview responses. They were considering the proper "fit" for me. I knew then that I had to go the extra mile.

As it was, I'd previously planned a post-holiday vacation in a neighboring state. I emailed the contact person and informed him that I would be vacationing nearby and that I would welcome the opportunity to drop by his office to meet the members of the team. I knew that this would be another chance to interview with them, so I dressed appropriately for the meeting.

158

I arrived a few minutes early and conversed with the receptionist. One by one, I met team members, as they returned from lunch. My time with the Division Head was limited, due to a critical meeting called by the State Superintendent. I'd learned years ago to have my "elevator speech" ready to go, and I delivered it in less than two minutes.

I later learned that my future colleagues were impressed with my instant rapport with everyone I met that afternoon. And what is more, they were impressed that I took the initiative to arrange a meeting with them. Later that afternoon, I was informed that the Division Head had authorized my employment as a School Transformation Coach. I'd gone the extra mile.

Well, the story didn't end there. Almost a month after the meeting, I still didn't have a contract or any tangible indication that I would be employed by the state department of education in the near future. I came close to giving up on the opportunity; then I remembered that I needed to persevere and go the extra mile. I sent an electronic message to the contact person, informing him of my continued interest in the School Transformation Coach position. He thanked me, saying that things were still in the works.

A few weeks later, I was in the state on personal business. I was standing knee deep in mounds of artwork, furniture, and paperwork, when my cellular phone rang. "Dr. Burks, I have your salary offer paperwork now, and I'd like to fax it to you, for your signature."

I knew I needed to go the extra mile, and I didn't miss a beat. "You won't believe it, but I'm in the state, moving things I left here years ago into storage. I'm less than 40 minutes away from your office, and if the team is willing to overlook how I'm dressed, I'll drive over and sign the document in person." Needless to say, when I arrived minutes later, the team was impressed, since I lived 2,000 miles away from the office!

Here's what I know for sure. In this age of permanent whitewater, when things are constantly shifting, it is imperative that those who are interested in leadership positions

> In this age of permanent whitewater, when things are constantly shifting, it is imperative that those who are interested in leadership positions persevere and go beyond the typical and every day.

persevere, and go beyond the typical and every day. Go the extra mile.

Tony Lamair Burks II
Superintendent-in-Residence,
National Center for Urban School Transformation
and School Transformation Coach

After five years as an elementary and middle school assistant principal, I felt I was more than ready to "take the helm" of a school, as a principal. I applied at one of the largest districts in Orange County, California. A good friend of mine was the assistant superintendent in this district, so I felt I had a slight advantage over the other candidates.

I rushed to the interview in the middle of a very hot summer day. I arrived with barely enough time to rush into the Human Resources office to face my interview panel.

I brought my suit jacket and left it in the car. Surely, they wouldn't expect me to wear a suit jacket, when it's 95 degrees, and I'm on the verge of sweating profusely. After all, I was wearing a nice dress shirt and my red "power tie." The interview went very well, and I felt like I "nailed it!"

Later that afternoon, I got a call from my friend, the assistant superintendent in this district. She told me the panel members said I did a great job in the interview, and my answers were "right on." Then she asked me some questions.

Did I own a suit with matching slacks and jacket? Was I trying to grow a trendy goatee? Finally, why were my keys hanging from a clip on my belt loop?

My friend was not on the interview panel, but obviously the members of the panel had told her they had concerns about my appearance. I was frustrated and defensively accused the panel of being "stodgy" and of misjudging me.

I angrily told my friend the panel should have judged me, based on the content of my answers, not on a few minor issues with my appearance. She replied with one simple sentence:

"The panel members feel they can find someone who is the 'whole package!'"

I believe we learn more from our failures than our successes. Since that day, I arrive to interviews early enough to cool off in the air conditioning, and put on my matching jacket. I also make sure that I am clean shaven, because someone on the interview panel may be from a different generation, and think my goatee isn't so trendy. I also unhitch my keys from my waist belt. It's all in the details, and after all, I'm competing with others, who are the "total package!"

> **I believe we learn more from our failures than our successes.**

As an aspiring administrator, I remember feeling defeated and saying to a colleague/mentor, "It's obviously not meant to be!" My colleague replied, "It's not that it's not meant to be...it's just not meant to be easy." Those words stuck with me, as I realized I would need to increase my determination and knowledge, regarding how to best "package" my abilities in a highly competitive field. It's all about perseverance, packaging, and preparation!

Dr. Preston Perez
Middle School Principal

Parting Shots

Now that you are finishing the book, I am confident you have the information needed to formulate a game plan, engage in an ongoing self-promotional effort, and develop a regimen of practice that will enable you to deliver an opening interview statement with a smile.

Success depends not only on getting an interview but delivering a professional performance that demonstrates you have what it takes to lead. By showcasing your abilities and sharing stories that confirm that you care about students, value relationship building, and know how to build teams, employers will recognize you as the candidate they truly want to work with.

Take some comfort in knowing that getting a promotion is a difficult process, and success only comes with patience and perseverance. In writing on perseverance, Pat Clark White summarizes the job interview process very well:

> *On any given day, one horse is going to be a nose faster than all the others, and it's not always the same horse. It depends on many factors in that particular race.*

I have attempted to share some of those subtle factors to take with you into the race; factors you need to give you the competitive edge.

I have shared many of my personal experiences with you, in the hopes that you can learn from them.

What I learned in writing this book is how hard I worked to gain these top spots of leadership. At the time, I found the wins thrilling and invigorating, and the losses devastating. But every job application and interview contributed to making me a better educator and leader. I learned how to overcome defeat and learned from my mistakes. Most importantly, I listened to mentors, who took time to guide me through some challenging times. I have taken key elements from the job search process and packaged them for you to use on your own journey.

I have known many educators, who should have been promoted but weren't, due to various factors, such as lack of confidence or clear sense of direction. Many qualified educators are not aware that they have the potential to lead. They have not had the encouragement from a friend or a mentor, who would tell them they have the potential to do more, pull them out of their comfort zone, and help them attain the next level in their career. This has always upset me, because so many in our field are intelligent, creative thinkers, and demonstrate leadership potential. As we approach what I believe to be the "Perfect Storm" in our public school system, we will need to recognize these "latent leaders" from our ranks, and encourage them to take on new and more challenging roles.

As a person with a desire to grow and a critical awareness of what it takes to succeed, now is the time to make your move. I sincerely believe that working as an educational leader is one of the most rewarding careers in the world. I wish you all the best on your journey.

~ *Marilou Ryder*

ABOUT THE AUTHOR

As an educational leader, Dr. Marilou Ryder has had the opportunity to participate in a wide range of experiences, at both the site and district levels. Working in six school districts and two states, her experiences include classroom teaching and site administration, at the secondary level. She served as an assistant superintendent of educational services and district superintendent, for both unified and union high school districts.

Marilou holds a Master's degree from Syracuse University and received her Doctorate in Educational Administration from the University of La Verne. In addition, she pursued post-graduate studies at the University of California, Irvine and CSU, Long Beach. Dr. Ryder also served as an adjunct instructor for CSU Fullerton, teaching graduate courses in leadership, governance, and school finance. She currently teaches organizational leadership for Brandman University, part of the Chapman University system.

Active in dialogue on educational policy issues, Dr. Ryder has worked with groups statewide to promote public education. An accomplished presenter, she speaks before numerous education groups, retreat groups, leadership organizations, and service clubs. Her leadership roles have included participation in educational women's mentoring groups and serving as a board member for various educational foundations. In 2007, Dr. Ryder was named "Top Ten Business Professional Women of the Year" for her involvement in local community affairs.

Throughout her career, Marilou has been an energetic and determined advocate for children, committed to raising the quality of education through comprehensive and sustained reform. Her priorities include raising academic standards through accountability, making sure every child graduates from high school, improving the quality of principals and teachers, ensuring that schools are safe and healthy places for learning, and increasing the support of parents and communities in public schools.

Under her leadership, Calle Mayor Middle School in the Torrance Unified School District was recognized as a California Distinguished School and National Blue Ribbon School of Excellence. Her colleagues recognized her leadership, by selecting Dr. Ryder for the California Administrator of the Year Award and the Johns Hopkins Outstanding Administrator.

As a Superintendent for two school districts, Dr. Ryder has instituted important change issues. Recent accomplishments include: (1) significantly improving student achievement and engagement; (2) establishing an Early College Campus; and (3) launching a virtual high school.

Recently retired, Dr. Ryder established Ryder and Associates, an educational consulting firm, dedicated to providing leadership services to schools and individuals. Her services include executive mentoring, in which she works with clients to develop self-promotion plans, write strategic cover letters, design powerful resumes, and engage in focused and deliberate interview preparation. Results include higher career performance and increased confidence in her clients' ability to gain promotions.

Dr. Ryder would be delighted to speak to your group on the subject of *Rules of the Game: Winning a Job in Educational Leadership*. Contact her for availability.

Dr. Marilou Ryder
Marilou@Ryder-Associates.com
www.Ryder-Associates.com
760-900-0556 (Cell)